THE SOUNDTRACK OF LEADERSHIP

The Soundtrack of Leadership

What Music Teaches Us About Leadership and Culture

Karlton Butts

Published by Game Changer Publishing

Paperback ISBN: 978-1-967424-72-6

Hardcover ISBN: 978-1-967424-73-3

Digital ISBN: 978-1-967424-74-0

www.GameChangerPublishing.com

First, I'd like to dedicate this book to my wonderful parents, Thomas and Janie, and my two older brothers, Derrick and Steve, who provided the foundation for my connection with music.

Second, I'd like to dedicate this book to my amazing wife, Kelley, who shares my passion for music and continues to inspire and motivate me every day.

Third, I'd like to dedicate this book to my friends for being an important part of my musical journey, whether we jammed together in a band or simply shared memorable moments through music.

Lastly, I'd like to dedicate this book to you, the reader. I hope you enjoy reading it as much as I enjoyed writing it!

READ THIS FIRST

Just to say thanks for buying and reading my book, I would like to give you some free gifts!

The Soundtrack of Leadership Community

This QR code leads to a paid online community to connect with me and other leaders who share a passion for music. People who purchase the book will receive one month free.

The Soundtrack of Leadership - Exercises and Workbook

This QR code leads to a workbook that includes all of The Soundtrack of Leadership exercises and space to answer questions, take notes, and reflect thoughts.

Five Leadership Lessons I Learned from Playing In a Band (BONUS VIDEO)

This QR code leads to a video of me providing five leadership lessons I learned from playing in a band.

THE SOUNDTRACK OF LEADERSHIP

WHAT MUSIC TEACHES US ABOUT LEADERSHIP AND CULTURE

KARLTON BUTTS

FOREWORD

Never has my Alexa been so busy as when I was reading *The Soundtrack of Leadership*. Every few minutes, I found myself asking it to play music by a particular artist or, as Karlton described, some aspect of the history of a band to illustrate a leadership principle. This was the first time my inquiry into leadership had a soundtrack. This was both a trip down memory lane and an opportunity to think about leadership in a new way.

If I am being completely honest, until I read *The Soundtrack of Leadership*, I had never really understood that bands might have visions and missions, as well as operating principles and guidelines. It had not occurred to me that the journey from asking friends to play music in your garage, to a first gig, to an album, to touring—and sustaining that, is parallel to starting a company in your basement, bringing on some staff, getting an office, and developing a long-term business strategy. Of course, leadership characteristics are at play! And, of course, these are relevant to all leadership situations.

When I met Karlton in 1984, I was drawn to his warmth, sense of fun, and absolute love of music. Young men in college in the 1980s were not famous for being thoughtful or sensitive. Karlton not only wore these attributes well, but he also inspired others to be better. At the same time, he was easy with a laugh, and with his unrivaled (in my experience) ability to rap off-the-cuff, he was fun to be around. I did not grow up in a musical household, but being around Karlton and his friends brought me to many live musical performances and exposed me to all kinds of new music (what we now call classic rock!). And I got to see Karlton as the leader of a band.

He was the first—and only—person to ever ask me to be in a band. Maybe now, in the era of autotune, I could have taken him up on it. But back when your voice was your voice, there was no hope for me. I really appreciated this vote for my attitude over my abilities! I will also never forget the time Karlton substituted my name into the song "Rock me Amadeus," singing "Sean O'Brien, Sean O'Brien, rock me Sean O'Brien" live, on-stage, as a going away present when I left for my junior year of college abroad.

As often happens, life gets in the way of friendship. This is not exactly right… it puts gaps in friendships, and if the friendship is deep and true, the passage of time does not matter. Karlton and I drifted apart as I studied abroad, and he transferred to a different college when I returned. After college, we lived in different parts of the country and pursued very different career paths—him as an engineer, lawyer, and entrepreneur (and musician, of course), and me as an ecologist and nonprofit executive.

We had both been successful in our careers, loved our families, and been busy with all that life throws at a person. However, when we got back in touch, we picked up so naturally that I wonder about the hole that existed in my life for all those years without him in it. Amazingly, we had also made a change in our lives at nearly the same time to pursue coaching and leadership development.

In addition to my repeated trips to the "vinyl" that *The Soundtrack of Leadership* initiated, *Soundtrack* was also a refreshing approach to talking about leadership lessons for people in all fields. I have read dozens of books and articles about leadership. Occasionally, musicians or bands have been used as examples, but this was my first exposure to a fully developed set of ideas and principles focused on how leadership plays out in bands and then how these principles can apply to your professional life (even for a non-musician like me).

I am glad I read this book and can now appreciate a whole new aspect of the implementation of sound leadership principles. Many parts of this book resonated with me, in particular, Karlton's emphasis on creativity, curiosity, and communication. In the context of the music world, these concepts seem obvious, yet in the moments when leadership is needed, it is easy to lose sight of key principles. I appreciated the reminders and examples in *Soundtrack*, and I will strive to keep them in mind as the rest of my world tour continues.

Finally, Karlton brings incredible passion to the subject of leadership and music. His encyclopedic knowledge of music is evident, as is his love of the creative process. It is wonderful to peek into a person's passion. Following Karlton's advice, I am making my soundtrack of the songs I consider to be essential—like old friends.

Alexa, play "Rock Me Amadeus."

Sean T. O'Brien, Ph.D.
Founder of Jeito Collaborative, Co-Founder of Sparrow Leadership, Host of
Finding Jeito Podcast

CONTENTS

INTRODUCTION

Who am I, and how did I get to where I am today? Well, first and foremost, I love music. From a young age, I was always drawn to music in many ways. It was all around me—whether it was music played at home, in the car, or while hanging out with friends. Music from television shows and movies also caught my attention. I always noticed music and focused on how it made the world around me better.

I started performing music at a young age. I sang in a youth choir and played clarinet and saxophone in school. But my connection with music reached a new level once I started learning to play guitar. My first experience with the guitar was short-lived. My mom found a guitar teacher in my hometown in Connecticut, and I began taking lessons every week. Initially, I didn't like it. I liked the guitar itself and the idea of being good at playing it one day, but I didn't enjoy the lessons or the practicing. My teacher was great and did everything he could to help me learn, but I was distracted. At that age, I just wanted to have fun, which meant hanging out with my friends and playing sports.

My other issue was the theory. Don't get me wrong; music theory is important. I didn't fully understand its value, though, until college. But I realized that I had an ear for music. I could hear a song and figure out how to play it on the guitar faster than I could learn the theory and read the notes from a page. Another benefit of having an ear for music was that I could *feel* the music—something difficult to capture when simply reading notes. That *feeling* is what I believe drew me to music from such a young age.

Eventually, my interest in hanging out with friends and playing sports won out, and I quit taking guitar lessons. After that, I didn't think about the guitar much—until I started listening to rock music with my friends in high school. The guitar in that music stood out to me and captured my attention. Classic rock and '80s rock were heavily guitar-driven, and I loved listening to the solos. I realized I had a passion for guitar all along—I just needed the right music to bring it out.

I started playing guitar again. I still didn't want to take lessons, so I taught myself. I soon became obsessed with it. I would get *Guitar Player* magazine, read about the great guitarists, and learn about new gear. My first electric guitar was a Fender Stratocaster, and I believe my first amp was a Crate. As my skills improved, I regularly stopped by a local guitar shop to check out new gear.

That's when I stumbled upon a guitar made by Schecter Guitar Research, an American manufacturer. If you're not familiar with them, the music video for the song "Eminence Front" by The Who (this was in the '80s) features Pete Townshend playing a black Schecter telecaster-style guitar. The craftsmanship of these guitars was amazing, so I custom-ordered one with a white stratocaster-style body and black hardware through my local guitar shop.

I ended up playing that Schecter guitar throughout my high school and college years, but after many years of endless modifications, I sold it. In hindsight, I should have kept it in its original form. That guitar would be a collector's item today and worth much more than I paid for it. I really do miss that guitar.

Now that I had a guitar I liked, I needed an equally impressive amp to go with it. Through extensive research—mainly reading reviews in *Guitar Player* magazine—I found an amp made by a company called Mesa Boogie that was in my price range. The amp was the Studio .22 model, and the closest store that sold it was Manny's Music in New York City. If you were in the music scene in the New York area, then you knew Manny's.

To a kid from Connecticut like me, it was the Disney World of music equipment—a magical place. When it closed in 2009, I was sad to see it go.

As I got better at playing guitar, I had aspirations of making it in the music business and one day being featured in *Guitar Player* magazine! Now, I'll admit the first few bands I played in weren't all that great. Once I got a taste of playing guitar in front of an audience, though, I was hooked. That was all I wanted to do. The connection made with people through music is intoxicating. Seeing their faces light up when I play a song they love is an amazing feeling. It's powerful to watch an audience get up out of their seats to dance and sing along. I believe life is about moments, and helping to create special moments for others through music is one of the best experiences ever.

When I went to college, I started playing out more and meeting other musicians. I played in a few different bands, and I couldn't get enough. Even though I played guitar, if a band needed a bass player, I would join and play bass—anything to get back on stage in front of an audience.

My aspirations to make it in the music industry were interrupted in college when I became very ill. While I survived the illness, it refocused my priorities in life. I realized I needed a career to fall back on if music didn't work out. So, I transferred colleges and dove headfirst into electrical engineering. I excelled in this field. After my first year at my new college, I was near the top of my class and secured a summer internship with NASA doing flight simulation. While I still played in bands, my main focus was on getting my degree. The internship at NASA checked multiple boxes for me: It was a great opportunity to apply what I had learned in my electrical engineering classes, and it also aligned with one of my other passions: aviation.

My dad flew airplanes as a hobby, and he introduced me to flying at a very young age. I loved every minute of it. He took me to airshows in the Northeast and other cool places like Nantucket (an island in Massachusetts) and Hershey, Pennsylvania. I would fly with him every chance I could. The following summer, I had an opportunity to intern at McDonnell Douglas in St. Louis, Missouri. At McDonnell Douglas, I worked on the F/A-18 Hornet fighter jet assembly line doing artificial intelligence and robotics. Of course, given my passion for music, I sought out other musicians in the internship program to form a band—and we did. It really made that summer special.

I enjoyed my first internship at McDonnell Douglas so much that I returned the following year for a second internship focused on engineering contract services. I had an idea that I might want to go to law school, so this position gave me some insight into what it was like to work in the legal profession. Later that summer, I spent a week in Cambridge, Massachusetts, attending the Harvard Business School Summer Venture in Management program. I talked with administrators from the business and law schools, and my interest in the latter received a further boost. At that moment, I made up my mind about which direction I'd take.

Before going to law school, though, I needed to earn some money to pay for it, so I accepted a consulting position at Booz Allen Hamilton which, at the time, was located in Bethesda, Maryland. This opportunity helped me learn about working with clients to understand how their businesses operate, collaborating with leaders to address challenges impacting their industries, and developing effective solutions that enhance growth.

I eventually went to law school at George Washington University Law School in Washington, D.C., and became an attorney. After working at a couple of law firms in the Washington, D.C. area, I wanted to focus more on entertainment law because of my passion for music. So, my wife and I moved to Los Angeles, where I joined a large firm that handled entertainment and intellectual property law. Working in another region and with clients in the entertainment industry was an exciting part of my journey.

I ended up leaving law firm life to work as an in-house attorney for a video-on-demand startup. The opportunity to work at a startup on the cutting edge of entertainment and technology was intriguing. It really opened my eyes to new media and the surge of digital film and music. It was an incredible experience being at the forefront of this new era of technology—and doing it with an amazing group of people didn't hurt. Of course, a few of us formed a band and played at our holiday party. It was an awesome night! Our setlist included both classic rock and hip-hop.

From there, I worked at a publicly traded company focused on licensing. As senior vice president, I primarily focused on generating revenue for the company. However, the experience also allowed me to work with innovators and be involved in developing state-of-the-art technologies.

When I left that role, I became an entrepreneur, working on several startups, including serving as CEO of an artificial intelligence and machine learning company. Ultimately, I wanted to help people. I wanted to help business leaders grow revenue and profitability while improving their leadership and culture. I also wanted to work on projects that involved music. I formed my coaching and consulting company, Mattertree, to pursue both objectives. I use my experience as an engineer, attorney, and business executive to help leaders and companies excel. And, in some cases, I do it through people's inherent connection with music. (We'll talk more about this in the next section.)

With Mattertree, I help leaders and businesses through coaching and consulting while also providing fun and engaging workshops to help organizations overcome challenges in performance and productivity. Whether it's assisting organizations to be more innovative, adding clarity to vision and growth, or aligning teams with a company's goals and objectives, I'm committed to serving individual and organizational success. I try to incorporate music into my work any chance I get, because of its transformational power to help people learn and to help bring people together.

And what really brings me joy is connecting with people—whether I'm meeting someone new in an airport or giving a keynote on stage. I still feel the magic and excitement that I felt when I was a teenager in a band connecting with audiences. In fact, those feelings are stronger than ever. The only difference is that instead of playing guitar in a band, it's me with a mic in my hand. The goal is the same: to make our moment together memorable and rewarding. That is the inspiration behind this book. And that is where I am today.

So Why Did I Write This Book? (And Why Should You Listen to Me?)

My aim in this book is to use music and people's deep connection with it to help them become better leaders, colleagues, and people. I meet executives and business leaders all the time who share impactful stories about music. Some played an instrument in high school or college. They tell me stories of how music has changed or improved their lives. How it helps balance the chaos between work and family, and how it has created lasting friendships and new experiences along their life's journey.

It's amazing to meet new people with a similar passion for music. That's who I wrote this book for.

I've been fortunate to have a successful career across multiple industries and sectors—working in government, professional service organizations, and private and public companies, from startups to large corporations. I've been in entry-, mid-, and senior-level positions, and I've worked as a CEO, so I've seen and experienced a lot over my career. Throughout my professional journey, I have encountered many different leadership styles—some effective, some not. I've also seen both healthy and toxic business cultures. In most instances, I observed and took mental notes on what was working, what wasn't, and where help was needed. I've also made my own mistakes as a business executive and leader—we all have—but I've learned from each of them.

This is not a how-to book, nor is it intended to offer business or legal advice (that's the attorney in me speaking). I am simply sharing my observations, experiences, stories, and lessons learned in business and leadership—using music to make it fun and engaging. If this book helps you and your business somehow, then I've done my job. If it takes you back to special moments in your life or reminds you of stories that involve music, then mission accomplished. If it simply gets you to revisit your playlist and think about old friends, I'll be happy. Maybe you'll even pick up the phone and call a few of those friends to reminisce.

Hopefully, this book does all of that while also providing practical insights you can apply in your day-to-day business as a leader to optimize performance and productivity and achieve your company's goals and objectives.

If you finish reading this book, I hope to meet you one day. I would love to hear about your music journey and how this book helped you. Knowing that this book resonates with others who are passionate about music will make all the effort of writing it worthwhile. This was a passion project for me—to help others succeed and become better people through music. I hope I've accomplished that.

We are all different and have an individual, personal connection with music. In this book, I am giving you a glimpse into my music journey. As you read about mine, think about your own music journey—your favorite songs and bands and moments where music has touched your life.

Be open-minded as you read this book. Think about how the songs in your playlist have shaped your life and created incredible memories for you and the people you've connected with. Sharing that connection with others can be liberating and create lifelong friendships. Think of the music you love and apply some of the parallels I draw between how music impacts our personal lives and how it connects us emotionally, physically, and spiritually. Think about how music has shaped your life. Taking this approach will allow you to get the most out of this book and help you become a better leader and person, for yourself and for those around you.

I've structured this book to take you on a journey through the evolution of a band and how that journey parallels the evolution of a leader and the growth of an organization. I will share anecdotes and experiences that have influenced my life both personally and professionally. I'll also share stories I've come across over the years that have resonated with me and offer context to some of the lessons I've learned along the way.

This book is divided into **Ten Pillars**—each representing an important milestone in the evolution of a band and how that evolution corresponds to being an effective leader, creating a high-performance culture, and building a successful organization. For that reason, I encourage you to read the chapters in order to see how each pillar unfolds and provides the foundation for subsequent chapters.

The journey begins with our first chapter, which explores how music connects us emotionally and universally-starting at a young age with our family and friends, and evolving over time as we meet new people and encounter new experiences.

PART I
PILLAR ONE: OUR
RELATIONSHIP WITH MUSIC

1
THE UNIVERSAL LANGUAGE OF MUSIC

*I*magine your favorite song playing. How does it make you feel? What memories come to mind when you hear it? Who do you see in that memory? Where were you the first time you heard that song? How many times have you listened to it? Do you know the lyrics, the melody, the iconic hook, riff, or solo? How does it move you? How does it affect your mood? Does it make you smile, cry, dance, or sing aloud? Does it give you energy or motivation? Does it give you a sense of power or confidence?

Oftentimes, it's not just about the song—it's about the artist as well. What is it about that artist or band that you like? How do they make you feel? What is it about them that appeals to you? What is it about them that you see in yourself? How do you connect with them—not just through their songs but through everything else they do? Their presence on social media, their merch, how they carry themselves in public, how they interact or collaborate with others, and the causes they stand up for. What about them makes you feel so connected that they play such an important role in your life? Maybe it's their image, attitude, energy, or skills. Or maybe you want to be like them—to live the life of a rock star with all the fame, success, and money.

The answers to these questions reveal how deeply we connect with

3

music, yet we don't really stop to think about it. Sometimes, music is just in the background—we expect it when we watch a TV show or a movie or when we're at the gym. Whether consciously aware of it or not, the reality is that we all have a deep, personal connection with music. It plays a profound role in our lives.

But it's not just about our relationship with a song or an artist. It's also about how that song or artist connects us with other people—emotionally, physically, and universally.

I can share an example with you. My wife and I traveled to Jamaica for a long-needed vacation. We were on a bus from the airport to our hotel when Bob Marley's song "Waiting in Vain" started blaring on the radio. Suddenly, all of us on the bus started tapping our toes, moving our hands to the beat, and humming along. We were a group of strangers—from different walks of life and parts of the world, speaking different languages—looking forward to our vacations, brought together by the music.

In that moment, I realized the true power of music—how it is a universal language that connects us globally. It doesn't matter where you're from, what culture you grew up in, or what your favorite songs are. There is always music, in different languages and from different cultures, that can affect you and connect you with others in some way.

To me, music is truly the soundtrack of our lives. It profoundly influences how we see and experience the world, defining moments in our lives, whether we're alone or with others.

And that connection starts when we're young. I think of parents singing to their babies while holding them, looking at them lovingly, or sharing songs that have impacted their lives. It's the beginning of a parent passing down songs from their personal soundtrack to the next generation. And even if they're not singing, they're humming or playing music in the background. These moments allow children to learn about music, experience its beauty, and develop a relationship with it that will likely influence their lives.

As we grow, music continues to shape us. Growing up in Connecticut, my first memories of music started in church, where I would listen to the choir and feel the passion in each voice. I especially enjoyed songs with a lead singer because they would go back and forth with the choir as if they were talking to each other through the music.

At home, my parents mostly played R&B—The Temptations, Gladys Knight & The Pips, The Staple Singers, Sam Cooke, Teddy Pendergrass, Al Green, Stevie Wonder, and Jackie Wilson. I loved listening to such moving music and could feel the emotion of the singers and musicians coming through the speakers. I quickly understood why they called it *soul* music. My older brothers played Earth, Wind & Fire, Kool & the Gang, Prince, Heatwave, and other great R&B artists from the '70s and '80s.

There was also a radio station in New York City I used to listen to called WBLS. We could barely get the signal, but it was my introduction to rap—The Sugarhill Gang, Grandmaster Flash, Kurtis Blow, Run-D.M.C.—and a broader range of R&B, including The Isley Brothers, Sly and the Family Stone, and Parliament-Funkadelic. It was very different from what my friends at school were listening to.

Growing up, my best friend had a car, and he played rock and metal music everywhere we went. He introduced me to bands like Van Halen, AC/DC, and Judas Priest. Other friends introduced me to bands like Journey, Rush, and Def Leppard. I didn't often listen to these bands at home, but over time, I learned to appreciate this genre of music. And I wasn't sure why, but it was music I wanted to keep listening to and learn more about. Little did I know at the time that rock music would have a big influence on my music journey. Being exposed to a variety of music at a young age helped me appreciate all the different types of music out there. I realized that even if you favor one particular genre, songs from all genres can move you and connect with you in some way. I was fortunate to learn at an early age that *a good song is a good song,* no matter the genre.

Music's influence on me didn't come just from audio—it also came from television and movies. Music from kids' shows like *Sesame Street* and *Schoolhouse Rock* had an impact on me. As a kid, you learn the lyrics to the songs, you experience the music with friends, you sing along, you tap your toe. However it happens, you develop a connection with the music and the characters and the images you see on screen. The music plays as significant a role as the visuals in helping you connect with a particular show or character, strengthening the whole experience. I knew every word from those *Schoolhouse Rock* cartoons and still remember some of them to this day—I'll never get "I'm Just a Bill" out of my head.

Another major influence on me was the cartoon *A Charlie Brown Christmas*. When I watched it for the first time, I connected with the music immediately. To me, it truly brought the characters and scenes to life. I didn't know what type of music it was when I first heard it, but it was my first real exposure to jazz. After hearing Vince Guaraldi's music in that cartoon, I wanted to listen to more of his work and explore other jazz artists like him.

As I got older, I started picking up on commercial jingles, TV theme songs, and movie soundtracks. I'll never forget the catchy jingles from McDonald's, Kit-Kat, and Dr. Pepper, or the theme songs from TV shows like *Sanford and Son*, *Good Times*, *Welcome Back, Kotter*, and *Cheers*. Then there were the soundtracks from movies of my youth, such as *Star Wars*, *Rocky*, and *Purple Rain*. The music from these examples connected me emotionally to what I saw on the screen. More modern examples include commercial jingles from Kay Jewelers and State Farm, theme songs from *Parks and Recreation*, *The Office*, and *Game of Thrones*, and the soundtracks for *Gladiator* and *Interstellar*.

Frequently, a song will catch our attention immediately. You'll hear a song for the first time that connects with you for some reason—but you don't know why. That feeling brings you back, making you want to listen, watch, or learn more. When I first heard the theme song from the TV show *Taxi* many years ago, I wanted to learn more about the artist. I later discovered it was the music of Bob James, one of the greatest jazz pianists of our time. Hearing the *Taxi* theme while watching a taxi drive across the Queensboro Bridge into Manhattan takes your imagination beyond the visuals on screen.

I recently had that same feeling while watching the TV series *Yellowstone*. They did an amazing job incorporating music into the show, especially in scenes featuring live performances. The music they selected connects you emotionally with the characters, the scenery, and the moment, immersing you in the storyline. That's the other beauty of music —not just hearing a song in its pure form but experiencing music that stimulates your imagination and takes you to another place.

As you find songs you like—whether from your favorite band, TV show, or movie—you start creating a mental playlist that reflects the soundtrack of your life. We can all relate to that. The second you hear the theme song for *The Office*, you immediately recognize it. The first few notes take you back to that show, bringing back memories of your favorite characters, episodes, and one-liners.

In some cases, it brings a smile to your face or even inspires you to go back and rewatch old shows—another way music plays such an influential role in our lives. Take *Game of Thrones*, for example. It's not music you would dance to, but it sets the mood for what you're about to watch. As a horror movie fan, I know music plays a major role in setting the mood. I'll never forget watching movies like *Jaws, Halloween,* and *Friday the 13th*—the eerie background music building anticipation for what would happen next. For example, when a character in a horror movie hears a creaking sound in the basement at night, and they're alone. They open the door and start walking down the basement stairs in the dark, gripping a knife, a skillet, or any other kitchen utensil they can quickly find. The creepy music starts playing, preparing the audience for what's coming—another example of how music connects you to that moment and immerses you in the storyline.

Music touches our lives in so many ways. When we work out, we often listen to music. It's playing in stores, elevators, and at parties. It's everywhere. And there's a reason: music influences our mood and behavior in those moments—sometimes even encouraging us to buy more!

One of the great things about hearing music wherever we go is that we can discover new songs and artists we might not have come across otherwise. We've all had those moments when we hear a song we didn't know before but immediately connect with. Shortly after moving to Los Angeles, I was invited to an event for City of Hope, a cancer research organization. Faith Hill was performing. I didn't know much about her then, but when I heard her sing "Breathe" live, I was blown away. Listening to her perform that song with such passion was an unbelievable experience.

And those are the moments when you find songs that resonate with you, even outside of your usual genre, and they become part of your personal playlist, expanding your musical interests. They become part of the soundtrack of your life because they take you back to a moment in time—memories you'll never forget.

A few years ago, I was shopping with my wife when I heard a song playing over the outdoor speakers. I didn't know what it was, but as soon as I heard it, I thought, *Wow, this is a great song.* I did everything I could to figure out what it was. I'm sure you've been there—you hear a song and get on Google or Shazam to find out who sings it. But sometimes, you just don't know. I searched online, hummed into Shazam, trying every possible way to identify the song, but nothing came up.

We were out shopping again not long after that, and I heard the same song playing again. This time, I was able to Shazam it. It turned out to be "Ain't It Fun" by Paramore. At the time, I wasn't really familiar with Paramore, but that song in particular made me want to learn everything I could about who sang it.

That's one of those experiences where a song connects with you in a certain way. It doesn't matter what genre it belongs to or who sings it—it's all about your emotional connection with that song at that moment. And for me, I connected immediately with "Ain't It Fun."

There are other universal experiences where you connect with artists outside your genre or culture. I've heard people say, for example, "I don't like country music," or some other genre or style. But I will tell you that some songs stand the test of time and can appeal to different audiences across generations.

One song I used to play on guitar many years ago was "Fast Car" by singer-songwriter Tracy Chapman. This song was released in 1988 and reached number six on the Billboard Hot 100 chart. In 2023, Luke Combs, a country artist, released his version of "Fast Car," which reached number two on the Billboard Hot 100 chart and number one on the Billboard Country Airplay chart. This song was written in a completely different era, for a completely different audience, and now it appeals to a new generation in a different culture and genre. And the song still has as much emotional impact today as it did in the '80s. You could even argue that it has a bigger impact now, given how well the song has done on Spotify and elsewhere.

It's a phenomenal song. Tracy Chapman and Luke Combs performed

"Fast Car" together at the Grammys in 2024. I think this was a pivotal moment in the culmination of the musical bridge that connects different generations and cultures influenced by that song. You can see they had genuine affection for each other, the song, and how they connected with the audience in that moment.

That's a great example of how music can transcend generations, cultures, races, and backgrounds. Music has the ability to bring all of us together and make people feel a certain way, no matter what style of music they're into.

Another way music connects people and brings them together is when we're in large groups, like at a sporting event. One example is singing the national anthem at a college football game. We all learned that song at a young age, and it's a very powerful one that unites us as a nation. It motivates us and inspires a sense of patriotism, and we also stand up, cover our hearts, and take our hats off. It evokes not only an emotional response but a physical one as well.

The national anthem is only the beginning. Throughout the country, stadiums play music to motivate fans of every sport. I've heard everything from Tom Petty's "I Won't Back Down" and The Killers' "Mr. Brightside" at football stadiums to "Take Me Out to the Ball Game" in the middle of the seventh inning at baseball games. This is just another example of how music can bring people from all backgrounds and walks of life together in a moment where they're all inspired and motivated to root for their team, salute their country, or bring more energy and life to the present moment.

When I think about how music makes us feel a certain way, I'm reminded of a quote by Maya Angelou:

"I've learned that people will forget what you said, people will forget what you did, but people will never forget how you made them feel."

This is such a powerful quote because it's so true in all aspects of life.

If people make you feel a certain way, you remember that. If they treated you with kindness or genuine affection, you remember that. If people treat you badly, you remember that too. It sticks with you, and it can damage or end your relationship with that person.

Sometimes, our favorite songs make us feel a certain way. One of my favorite songs is "I Can't Make You Love Me" by Bonnie Raitt. I could hear that song a million times, and it would make me feel the same way every time. But what's interesting is that when I mentioned this song to my good friend of twenty years, he said, "Wow, that's one of my favorite songs too." And I never knew that. We've been friends for so long but had never discussed this song until recently. When we realized we had similar tastes in music, it reinforced and created more positive moments in our friendship.

Music is about moments. After you bought your first car, you probably couldn't wait to play your favorite songs while cruising through the neighborhood. It truly is a time machine in the sense that you hear a song, and it can immediately take you back to a specific point in your life, bringing back good and bad memories. In an instant, music connects you with people, moments, and emotions as far back as you can remember. I cannot think of anything that impacts our lives more profoundly than music.

I don't think we spend enough time really thinking about music. It's something we hear and often take for granted. We think, *Okay, it's a song I like. I'll listen to it for the next five minutes and then move on to the next one.* But we rarely stop to consider what that song is actually doing to us.

Music influences us in ways we don't even realize, such as when someone is out in public humming under their breath. They're not consciously paying attention to the music, but you can tell it's triggering some kind of response in them, affecting their behavior in subtle ways. Sometimes, they may not even realize they're doing it, but the music is making them feel something or react in some way.

Music has the ability to make us move and, in some cases, do things we may not even intend to do. It reminds me of a skit from *Chappelle's Show* where Dave Chappelle and John Mayer went to different locations—a restaurant, a barbershop—to see how people from other cultures reacted when John played a song on his guitar. The skit played to stereotypes for laughs, but it really showed how certain music affects certain people and can make us move physically, even when we're not thinking about it. That was my takeaway from that skit, and I thought it was brilliant how it celebrated our cultural differences.

> **Exercise:** *Think about your favorite genre of music. What is it about this genre that deeply connects with you? Why do you love it? What about it resonates with you? How does it connect with your identity, emotions, or experiences?*

For example, some people have a deep love for country music; for them, it's more than just the music—it's an identity. If you walk into a country bar, you might see people dressed in cowboy hats and boots, fully embracing their connection with the music and with others who share that identity. Explore this for yourself as you do this exercise.

In the next chapter, we begin to examine how music and artists influence our lives, reflect our identity, and shape our leadership and vision.

2

MUSIC AS A MIRROR FOR LEADERSHIP

We can learn many leadership principles from our personal experiences with music. You can learn a great deal about a person just by looking at their playlist. Imagine walking up to a friend, colleague, or even your boss at work and saying, "Hey, could I take a look at your playlist?" As you scroll through, you might find songs that make perfect sense—songs that align with what you'd expect them to listen to. But then you may stumble upon something surprising that makes you think, *Wow, I didn't realize they would listen to that.* You might also be surprised by how many of their songs overlap with your own favorites.

I truly believe that a playlist is one of the most authentic reflections of who you are and what you love. I can't think of any other identifier that does this so clearly. But your playlist doesn't just reflect who you are when you create it—it also reflects your journey through life as you grow. Think about all the time and effort you put into curating your playlist. You intentionally start with the songs you know you love. That could be twenty, thirty, forty, or fifty songs—maybe more. But as you discover new music, you add songs to your playlist. And if you get tired of a song, you remove it. Every time you make those adjustments, it's a reflection of who you are at that moment in time, how your values change, and what influences your moods. Maybe you've evolved and no longer listen to certain songs or genres of music. Or maybe you've discovered a whole new genre, and now you're adding jazz, blues, classical, or some other style you hadn't explored when creating your playlist.

You'll add songs that inspire and motivate you, songs that prepare you for the day or help you take on a new challenge, songs that carry you through difficult times, or songs that make you feel a certain way in a specific moment. Discovering new songs can be a gift that keeps on giving. Even if you're listening to the song right now, you're also adding it to the memory of the moment you discovered it. You might think, *I can't wait to play this at my next pool party with friends,* or *I want to hear how this sounds cranked up in my car,* or *This would be a great song for my morning runs.*

Your playlist is the purest and most authentic reflection of who you are.

It also establishes your personal connection to the music and the artists performing it. Sometimes, it's about *who's* singing the song and how you relate to that particular band or artist. Growing up, a lot of kids put posters of their favorite bands or artists on their walls. Every time they walked into their room, those posters served as a reminder—*Oh, I love this band. I love Journey. I love Earth, Wind & Fire. I love Rick James.* Seeing those posters every day can reinforce a sense of identity and also deepen a connection with the artist.

I remember my first semester at the University of Virginia, meeting one of my neighbors in Echols Hall. He was from Stockton, California, and he was heavily into punk music. Growing up in Connecticut, I wasn't really exposed to punk music. I didn't listen to much of it, aside from *Blitzkrieg Bop* by The Ramones. None of my friends did, and no one in my family played punk music. The radio stations I listened to didn't play it. But when I met him, we talked about music, and he introduced me to a whole new world I hadn't yet discovered.

On his dorm room wall were posters of the Dead Kennedys, Butthole Surfers, Black Flag, and other popular punk rock bands. Those posters gave him an identity. Anyone who walked into his dorm room immediately knew what kind of music and bands he connected with, and the kinds of values he was likely to espouse, on the basis of the substantive content of the song's lyrics.

It's almost like fans take on the identity of their favorite artists. You see people dressing like punk rockers, hip-hop artists, or pop stars. The fact that an artist can create such a deep connection—beyond just their music—is incredibly powerful. In some cases, fans want to *be* them, or they shape their values around the artist's message. Sometimes we are drawn to bands because of our own felt or innate values. It's not like we're blank slates that simply absorb the message: we resonate with certain music and the messages it conveys (explicitly or implicitly), in a positive feedback loop.

For certain songs, the lyrics resonate so deeply that they influence how we see the world. We may not even think about it that way—we just say, *Oh, that's a cool band. I like their music, and I want to listen to them.* But often, they touch our lives in many ways—not only through their songs but through their style, artwork, posters, and even their merch. Fans wear their t-shirts and carry that identity with them. It isn't just about the song—it's about everything else the artist represents and stands for. You connect with their creativity. In some cases, you even see that creativity in yourself.

Music can unlock something inside you—something you may not have fully recognized before. But when you hear or see it, it's like, *Wow, that's me. I connect with that.* And it encourages you to bring that part of yourself into the world. It allows you to express a side of yourself that you may have kept hidden. Seeing other artists embrace their identity can give you the confidence to do the same—to proudly show your love for punk rock, jazz, or hip-hop.

As you go through your playlists and reflect on the songs you love, think about the artists as well. Consider what they stand for and how their messages align with your values. In some way, those artists and their music help shape your identity—who you are, what you stand for, and what you want to become. Again, take a holistic view—not just the music itself but also the band's image, their artwork, how they present themselves, and even how they speak.

We, as fans, aren't the only ones influenced by our favorite artists

—other artists are, too. Several British rock bands in the '70s emulated American blues artists like Muddy Waters and Howlin' Wolf. When American guitarist Jimi Hendrix first performed in England, he blew many British musicians away because they had never seen anyone play like him. Jimi's style, presence, and what he stood for inspired so many. Musicians took what they could from him and incorporated it into their own music and playing style. Many famous artists developed their unique sound by borrowing bits and pieces from others.

Similarly, you can take pieces of the songs in your playlist—songs that resonate with you—and let them shape your identity. Over time, your playlist reflects your values and who you are as a person. This naturally leads to how musical experiences shape leadership and vision.

> **Exercise:** *When thinking about your playlist and the music you love, ask yourself: How does it influence my mood, my attitude, my drive, and even my creativity?*
> - *Identify the characteristics within the songs that resonate with you—whether it's the lyrics, the melody, the tempo, the mood, or the style. That's what you're drawn to.*
> - *How do the qualities you connect with in those songs influence the energy you feel?*
> - *How do you reflect that energy onto others?*
> - *How does it shape how you interact with the people around you?*

These are important questions, especially in leadership and business. How you influence others plays a major role in how effective you will be as a leader. If you can't connect with people in a way that brings out the best in them, empowers them, and motivates them to achieve a shared mission, then that's something you'll need to work on. We'll explore these ideas further in this book.

Music can help unlock values and aspects of who you are, shaping your worldview, self-perception, and how you relate to others. It helps develop your value system, and I believe our playlists reflect that identity. They offer insight into what we value and how we see the world.

> **Exercise:** *What song has had the most impact on your life, and what is it about this song that deeply connects with you?*

Take the time to go through this exercise and reflect on your answer. Once you understand how you connect with one song on a deeper level, do the same with other songs you love. You'll start to see patterns in the songs that resonate with you. You may even be surprised by what you find, recognizing parallels between your music choices and your values. These values will shape who you are as a leader.

Don't just listen to music passively, as if it's background noise or something to tap your foot to. Ask yourself, *Why do I connect so deeply with this song?* If you take the time to do this, you'll learn so much about yourself and what truly defines you.

Some music is aggressive, like progressive metal, and maybe you listen to it because you connect with its intensity and attitude—that's how you see yourself or how you want others to see you. Maybe you're into hip-hop because you love its melodies, beats, and lyrical storytelling, and you relate to the culture through your upbringing or life experiences. Maybe you prefer positive, upbeat music that lifts your mood and makes you smile. Or perhaps you're drawn to heartfelt, emotional songs that reflect the struggles you've faced in life.

I think back to "I Can't Make You Love Me" by Bonnie Raitt. If you listen to the lyrics, the song tells the story of a woman experiencing a deep emotional struggle. She can't make the other person love her no matter what she does. That idea resonates because, in life, we all experience moments where we want to connect with someone, but for whatever reason, we just can't, no matter what we say or do.

That realization can be painful, but it teaches you how to shape your value system, how to respond to challenges like this, and how to move forward. Going through this reflection exercise can help you learn about yourself, how to overcome personal challenges, and how to better connect with others. Some people have lived through these moments and relate to them deeply. Knowing you're not alone in these struggles can help you work through them—and in some cases, even avoid them in the future.

As a leader in a company or an organization, you won't always connect with everyone on your team. You won't always see eye to eye with your peers, your boss, or others around you. So how do you handle that? You can't make them love you or even like you, but maybe there are other ways to build mutual respect, communicate effectively, and work together toward shared goals. Or perhaps you realize that it's time to part ways. Either way, you develop values that help you handle these situations authentically and consistently—values such as commitment, accountability, respect, loyalty, and courage.

And as we go through this book, we'll explore those ideas further. Again, music reflects these themes, and in some cases, it even prepares us —depending on how deeply we analyze the songs and how we relate to them. It can help us understand how to overcome challenges in real life.

So use music for more than just something to listen to and enjoy. Use it as a tool to learn about life and how to relate to people. You'll start to realize a few things. First, you'll understand why you like a particular artist—because they connect with you in a specific way.

But don't stop there.

Once you create those connections, use them as a way to reflect on yourself—on how you want to be perceived, how you want to project yourself to others, and how you can use that understanding to build better relationships, bond with more people, and grow into the best version of yourself.

In the next chapter, we'll explore how music relates to leadership specifically. By thinking about the bands you love and the musicians you respond to, we'll reflect on the leadership traits you've encountered and start to craft your own vision of what an ideal leader looks like—and the leader you aspire to be.

PART II
PILLAR TWO: THE MUSIC IN YOU

3

WHAT SONG DEFINES YOUR
LEADERSHIP STYLE?

*W*hat type of leader do you want to be?

Throughout our lives, we encounter countless leaders —whether they are our parents, teachers, principals, coaches, counselors, bosses, or others who have played a leadership role in shaping us. Over time, we observe their leadership styles, such as how they interact with people, how they handle crises, and how effective they are at bringing out the best in those they lead.

On a side note, we sometimes don't give our parents enough credit as leaders, considering everything some of us put them through growing up. But they are always trying to do what's best for us, even when we don't see it at the time. They usually focus on our long-term success, while we, in the moment, just want what we want—*now!*

In some cases, the leaders we admire are our favorite musicians. You might look at a bandleader like Prince, Tom Petty, George Strait, Hayley Williams, or Dave Grohl and feel a connection—not just to their music but to *them* as leaders. A lot of times, we're drawn in by the leader of the band just as much as the music itself.

But what is it about them that you see in yourself? And when you look at other bandleaders you admire, what traits do they have that reflect who you are or who you aspire to be? If you were leading a band, how would you inspire your bandmates to perform at their best? Maybe you'd lead through collaboration. Take Bono, for example—he's one of four members of U2, and they all write and perform together. But Bono is the frontman. He's the face of the band.

It's the same with the Rolling Stones or any other band you love—there's usually one or two leaders. What draws you to them? What do you like about their leadership style? It could be their ability to command an audience, how they interact with fans during a live show, how they speak in interviews, or how they carry themselves at events.

There are traits we pick up on—things we either recognize in ourselves or aspire to develop.

In the context of music, how would you be the best bandleader you could be? Would you ensure that everyone is in tune and stays in rhythm? That they show up on time for gigs and know their parts? That each band member plays a role in the songwriting process to make the song the best it can be?

How would you command an audience during a live show? What would you do to get the crowd engaged? Would you move around the stage? Would you have them sing along to certain parts of the song? How would you get them to react the way you want them to?

This is the chapter where we reflect on the leaders who have had the greatest positive impact on you—both in and outside of music. There are many examples of great leaders in music—artists who command the stage, interact with fans, and lead their bandmates. But let's also consider leaders from other areas of life.

What characteristics or traits have you admired in the leaders you've encountered over the years? Which of those traits would you want to develop in yourself?

Maybe you admire vocal leaders—those who are outspoken and direct. Or perhaps you respect leaders who lead by example, demonstrating through actions rather than words.

Maybe you gravitate toward leaders who focus on making each member of their team better so that success is shared by everyone. Or perhaps you prefer leaders who embrace curiosity, giving their team space to try new things, take risks, and fail—all in the pursuit of innovation.

Some leaders prioritize communication and feedback, encouraging creative input and ideas to strengthen the team and improve results.

Do any of these leadership styles resonate with you?

When I think of great artists as leaders, I'm reminded of a quote by Langston Hughes:

"An artist must be free to choose what he does, certainly, but he also must never be afraid to do what he might choose."

This quote resonates with me because if you want to succeed as a leader, you can't be afraid to make decisions and follow through on them with confidence.

In the context of music, as a leader, you want to inspire and motivate people—to push them toward a shared goal. You may choose a leadership style that doesn't appeal to everyone. When you make a decision after careful thought, you need to exhibit confidence and authenticity, even in the face of uncertainty or doubt.

You have to commit to your choices and remain true to yourself. Don't be afraid to be vulnerable. Don't be afraid to lead in a way that aligns with your values. Authenticity fosters trust between you and your team.

That's why this quote is so powerful. It reminds us that while choosing our path is important, we must also be fearless in following it, regardless of the outcome.

Having explored different leadership styles, we're now ready to begin thinking about how you can start developing your own.

To develop your authentic leadership style, take the time to assess your strengths and weaknesses, identify areas for growth, and create a realistic plan to reach your leadership goals.

If you're already leading a company, you should always be looking for ways to improve. What areas can you strengthen? How are you monitoring your progress to ensure you're as effective as possible?

Your self-assessment shouldn't just include *your* thoughts on how you can improve—it should also incorporate feedback from your team. One effective way to do this is through a **360-degree assessment**, where you gather input from your team members about what you're doing well and where you can improve. Honest feedback from those you lead can provide valuable insights and help you grow as a leader.

That's a powerful approach because you're actively listening to your team members and allowing them to give you feedback on how you can become a better leader. We all have blind spots; no matter how smart we think we are, great leaders understand their strengths and weaknesses.

They don't just acknowledge their strengths and weaknesses—they embrace them and take action accordingly. Leaders who believe they know everything and can solve every problem without anyone else's help are setting themselves up for failure. That mindset ignores the valuable input that could come from the team.

You want to be the kind of leader who gets the best out of everyone—whether they are outspoken and ambitious or striving to climb the corporate ladder. You may even have an employee who wants to come to work, do their job, and go home. Not everyone aspires to be a leader or a manager, and that's okay. Some employees are there to do their jobs well and contribute to the team in their own way. Recognizing these different roles is key. We'll discuss this further in later chapters, but an effective leader understands the importance of identifying the right people for the right roles.

Not everyone can be the lead guitar player. If you had a band with four lead guitarists and no drummer or bass player, you wouldn't have much of a band. You need people who embrace their roles, excel at what they do, and understand how their contributions make the entire band better.

Success isn't just about having the technical skills to play your instrument—it's also about knowing how to collaborate with and relate to the other band members. Whether you're writing songs, performing on stage, or going on tour, there are countless opportunities to bond with your bandmates and align with a shared vision. The leader's style plays a huge role in shaping those relationships and setting the tone for how the band evolves as a unit.

Look at what makes great leaders stand out, and think about how you can adopt some of those characteristics. Maybe it's your favorite artist, a leader you admire, or a combination of leaders you've encountered over the years. Identify the traits that resonate with you and that could help you become a stronger leader. Then, be proactive and plan your next steps with intention.

Great musicians learn from and are inspired by those who came before them. When I watched Prince perform, I could see traces of Jimi Hendrix in him—in the way he dressed, how he played guitar, and the overall energy of his performances. It was clear that Jimi was one of his influences. As a blues guitarist, one of my favorite artists was Stevie Ray Vaughan. If you look at Stevie Ray Vaughan's playing, you can see how he was influenced by Jimi Hendrix and blues legends like Albert King and Buddy Guy. But the beauty is that they didn't just imitate their predecessors—they took what they learned and made it their own. Stevie Ray Vaughan had an unmistakable style. The same goes for Prince—he was truly in a league of his own.

While he was undoubtedly inspired by others, he created an entirely new world of music through his songwriting, performances, and mastery of multiple instruments. Seeing Prince in concert was unbelievable—one of the best live performances I've ever witnessed. I honestly believe he was one of the most talented artists the world has ever seen.

Developing your leadership style is a lot like this music analogy. You're inspired by elements and traits from other leaders you admire—much like musicians drawing inspiration from the artists who came before them.

Your initial leadership style might look a lot like a cover band. Having been in several cover bands myself, I know that when you're in a cover band, you're playing music that someone else wrote, created, and performed. You're just replicating their work. There's not much authenticity in that sense—you're simply taking what someone else did and playing your version. Most cover bands try to play songs exactly as the original artist did because that's what the audience expects. Sometimes, you can take creative license and modify a song in a certain way, adding a personal touch. But initially, cover bands aim to sound as close to the original as possible.

In leadership, you may start out the same way—imitating those you admire, trying to match their style as you grow and develop. Ultimately, you want to create a leadership style that is unique and authentic to *you*. There's nothing wrong with learning from others, taking bits and pieces of leadership qualities you admire, or avoiding approaches that don't align with your values. You can learn from both the good and the bad and apply those lessons to your leadership journey. At the end of the day, you want *your own style*. I've seen some great bands cover Rolling Stones songs. But you don't just want to *sing* and *move* like Mick Jagger—you want to *be* Mick Jagger. That's the goal as a leader. You want to be authentic in your own right, create your style, write your own music, and forge your path.

We are all different, and we can rarely fake being someone we're not. So the key is to find a leadership style that allows you to be *authentic* while incorporating leadership traits that align with your values and inspire those around you to perform at their best.

This is where self-assessment comes in. You should always be asking yourself: *Am I being a good leader?* You should listen to the room. Pay attention to your team. Be aware of signs that indicate your leadership style isn't working—people tuning you out, losing trust in you, or disengaging from the mission. These issues can erode the foundation of a strong team, and a great leader must constantly be aware of them.

To truly improve, you need to look at where you are today. Assess your current leadership style. Gather feedback from your team and ask yourself, *What are three things I need to work on?* Once you've identified those areas, develop a plan or strategy to improve.

For example, let's say your team tells you that you're not a great listener. They feel unheard. You cut them off whenever they ask a question or shoot them down when they offer an opinion in a meeting. It's just a knee-jerk reaction, but you know you must overcome it to be an effective leader.

When you're the leader of a company, you're trying to hire the best and brightest people you can find—people who were at the top of their academic class, have demonstrated success in their prior roles, have won awards, or are otherwise highly regarded by their industry peers. Great leaders want to add high-quality people to their teams. But the worst thing you can do is bring them on board and not let them be great or not encourage them to be the best versions of themselves. You don't want to stifle them or impede their growth by imposing what you think is the right course of action instead of allowing them to offer input. You hired them for their expertise—let them voice their opinions and help shape the next direction for the team.

The reality is that in those instances—such as the example of not being a good listener—not only are you being an ineffective leader, but you're also stifling valuable input from your team. What I've seen over the years is that if you constantly cut people off, ignore their thoughts, or don't give them a chance to express their opinions, they will eventually stop offering them. They will stop asking questions. They will stop sharing their opinions. They'll think, *You know what? I'll just show up and do my job.* And now, despite spending all that money and effort recruiting the best and brightest, you're not letting them operate at their full potential.

You've essentially cut off their potential, preventing them from offering insights that could make you a better leader, improve your team, strengthen your products and services, or enhance how you serve your customers and audience. That's just one example of a leadership trait that needs to be recognized—through assessment and conversations with your team—and that requires intentional steps to improve.

One of those steps might be making a conscious effort not to cut team members off when they speak. Be intentional about listening. Let them finish what they have to say before offering your response. In these situations, I've seen people react defensively, especially when receiving criticism from a team member. Try to avoid that. Being a better leader doesn't mean vigorously defending your past decisions—because if your approach worked perfectly, your team wouldn't need to raise concerns. Instead of constantly defending your position, try saying, *Thank you, I'll consider that.*

Sometimes, you need to be vulnerable, set aside your ego, and acknowledge, *You know what? I can be better at that.* Taking intentional steps to improve, showing your team that you're listening, and demonstrating your commitment to making the team better will enhance your leadership and help build trust. That trust encourages your team to feel comfortable following your leadership. Beyond that, these habits will make you a better person outside of work as well.

When you embrace those leadership principles at work, they can also help you in life. Imagine if you could be a better listener at home—listening to your kids or your spouse more. In some cases, that might not always be easy, but at least you value their input and consider how to use it to improve the family as a whole. Who knows? Your kids might even see you as a better leader!

It's crucial to ensure that you are getting the best out of your team and that they view you as a leader with the highest integrity. Once again, you are applying the leadership traits you've observed or developed over time.

You want to create an authentic and sustainable leadership style that allows you to continue growing and evolving. Business conditions change constantly. Sometimes you're in crisis; sometimes you're thriving. The true test of a leader often comes not when things are going well but when they aren't. That's when you need to have your ear to the ground, actively listening to what your team is telling you to lead effectively. The same principle applies to your customers and audience.

You should regularly be gathering feedback, ensuring that your team feels heard and that communication remains open. When you take action to overcome challenges, you are considering the input from your team. This ongoing dialogue allows you to assess whether the steps you are taking to become a better leader are working.

Exercise: *Pick five songs that define you as a leader.*

List the leadership traits you identify in each song. For example, if you're listening to "Under Pressure" by David Bowie or "We Are the Champions" by Queen, what about that song resonates with you from a leadership perspective? Maybe it's a lyric, or maybe it's not even the words—perhaps it's something about the music itself that empowers you. The song's melody, rhythm, or emotion might move you in a way that fuels your leadership style.

Exercise: *Who do you think is the greatest frontman or band-leader of all time, and why?*

This ties back to our discussion about connecting with band leaders. Maybe you admire someone like Mick Jagger—you love his swagger, his style, his dance moves, and the way he sings and interacts with the audience. Maybe you appreciate his consistency as a leader and the energy he brings to the crowd.

This is important because, as a leader, you may have an audience—or a team—that has heard your messaging before. We'll discuss this in more detail later, but for now, you can think about how you can keep that message fresh. How do you keep them engaged and energized? How do you maintain their interest, even when delivering the same message repeatedly? That ability to keep things relevant and exciting is another valuable leadership trait.

You need to be intentional in how you handle those challenges, ensuring that everything you do as a leader resonates with your team and has the intended effect.

In the next chapter, we'll look at behaviors, attitudes, and limiting beliefs that are holding us back from performing at our best. We all have them. The question is: how can you identify and overcome these barriers to unlock your full potential as a leader? Read on to find out.

4

FROM BLUES TO ROCK

*W*e all have behaviors, attitudes, and limiting beliefs that hold us back. Breaking through those barriers will unlock a whole new version of yourself and allow you to reach your full potential. Many of us are accomplished, successful, and have done amazing things. But no one's perfect, and that will never change. You can strive to be as perfect as you want to be, but there will always be things that hold you back from becoming even better.

The goal of this chapter is to identify those obstacles and take steps to overcome them—unlocking new areas of growth where you can become a stronger leader and a better version of yourself. So, let's dive in.

We all engage in behaviors that hurt us, and in some cases, they define who we are. If you're always late to meetings, people notice. And if you're a leader, that's a serious problem. As a leader, you should always be early. Not only does chronic lateness reflect poorly on you, but it also impacts the team as a whole. If you have behaviors that negatively affect your leadership, you need to recognize and address those areas to become the best leader you can be.

Leaders face other challenges: overthinking, lack of planning, or poor decision-making. These behaviors must first be acknowledged as areas for improvement, and then intentional steps must be taken to overcome them.

In some cases, you might be self-aware enough to recognize that you're always late, or you might need feedback from your team to bring these issues to light. In addition to, or in lieu of, a 360-degree review, you might consider communication exercises or surveys to gather valuable insights from those you work with. But usually, deep down, we already know what our bad habits are. The biggest challenge is admitting they are a problem.

Once you can mentally accept that *I'm not perfect, I have things I need to work on, and I need to stop ignoring them,* you open the door to becoming a better leader. Recognizing that your strengths alone won't compensate for your weaknesses is key. Once you reach that point, you can start developing a plan for real growth.

To some extent, we all overthink. We consider multiple approaches to a problem, running through different scenarios in our minds. But sometimes, this leads to *analysis paralysis*—where you spend so much time considering options that you fail to act.

This doesn't just affect you as a leader—it impacts your entire team.

In business, time is money. Leaders must make quick, well-informed decisions that keep projects moving forward. Overthinking delays progress, slows innovation, and causes frustration.

Once you identify the behaviors holding you back, the next step is admitting, *This is a problem I need to work on.* And you're not alone—everyone has areas where they need to improve. No one is perfect. Get comfortable admitting your weaknesses. For example, you might say, *I know I'm a procrastinator. I know I need to get better. Now, I will focus on improving, be intentional about it, and build a support system to help me move past this.* Visualize what the "new you" will accomplish by overcoming this challenge. Think about how it will improve your life. Use this vision as motivation, knowing that the results you'll achieve will far outweigh the effort it takes to get there.

Another thing that can hold us back is our attitude. As Zig Ziglar said, *"It's your attitude, not your aptitude, that will determine your altitude."* So many people I've talked to have a negative attitude about themselves, their careers, their relationships, or life in general. No matter how they look at their situation, they don't see things positively. They say things like, "This will never work," or "I'm not doing that." It's completely self-defeating. The other day, I was talking to an actor who was telling me about a friend of his, also an actor. His friend is in great shape and maintains a disciplined workout schedule and diet to increase his acting opportunities. He finished his story by saying he could never do that: "There's no way I'm only eating once or twice a day."

I replied, "What you do depends on the goals you're trying to reach. Do you want to increase your acting opportunities? Set goals that will help you get there. Consider developing a workout schedule and diet that get the same results as your friend's but allows you to eat three balanced meals a day." With a negative attitude, you might not even consider this alternate path, and worse, you'll miss out on a lot of great opportunities.

The reality is that if you don't have a goal, then it's easy to say, "I would never do that," because you don't have a destination you're trying to reach. You're not actually trying to improve. You might still have dreams but no clear path to accomplish them.

If you haven't identified areas where you need to improve, then all your negative behaviors and attitudes will remain the same. You'll be stuck in a constant cycle of stagnation, wondering why you're not progressing. And now your soundtrack will be negative, full of complaints about what you don't want to do or aren't willing to try, instead of saying, *Okay, I don't like where I am. I'm stuck. I need to make these changes to get better. I'm going to set goals and take action.* And guess what? Your behaviors change. Your attitude changes. And now, all your energy is focused on improving your life, not wallowing in negativity.

Another thing that can hold us back is our limiting beliefs and perceptions. This includes thoughts like *I'm too old for this, I'm not smart enough,* or *I don't have time for that.* We all do it.

It's wired into our DNA. We all have fears of the unknown that influence our decision-making thought processes. This could be a fear of failure or, in some cases, even a fear of success. To recall the Langston Hughes quote from Chapter 3, "An artist must be free to choose what he does, certainly, but he also must never be afraid to do what he might choose." Maybe fear of success is just another limiting belief that holds us back. But it all goes back to what we discussed earlier—you need to at least acknowledge it as a problem.

We all fear failure. I remember performing with my band for the first time in front of an audience. All I could think about was, *What if we suck? What if I hit a bad note? What if I forget the lyrics? What if people look at us and think we're horrible, and they boo us off the stage?* That's a fear every band has the first time they play live, and honestly, you still feel it after the 100th show—it's just not as intense.

Leaders often grapple with limiting beliefs as well. What if you have a leadership idea or a direction you want to take, but you think, *I can never pull this off* or *I just can't make this work?* Another quote I live by is from Wayne Gretzky: "You miss 100% of the shots you don't take." You're almost hurting yourself more by not trying than you would be by trying and failing.

Most successful people you encounter—whether in business, sports, or any profession—have failed in some way on the path to where they are now. It's how you respond to failure that matters. You'll never grow if you let failure feed your negative attitudes and limiting beliefs. *Well, I tried it, but it didn't work. See, I'm not good enough. I'm not smart enough. This isn't working. I should never have tried in the first place.* And just like that, you fall back into negativity and start singing the blues.

I titled this chapter "From Blues to Rock" because blues songs often tell stories of the struggles people face in life. Blues music can be sad and heavy, but it can also be spiritual and uplifting. It's a genre that truly brings out deep emotions in people. Personally, I love blues music and play it every chance I get. If I'm having a bad day, I can pick up my guitar and play a few blues songs, and suddenly, my troubles seem to fade away. If you're a blues guitarist, you know exactly what I'm talking about.

I also enjoy listening to the blues because it has an emotional depth unlike any other genre of music. If you've ever listened to the Three Kings of Blues—Freddie King, Albert King, and B. B. King—or other blues guitarists like Eric Clapton, Buddy Guy, Stevie Ray Vaughan, or Derek Trucks, you can *feel* the emotion pouring through their fingers. Every note and every guitar lick speaks to you. In 2013, I attended Eric Clapton's Crossroads Guitar Festival at Madison Square Garden, and it was one of the best concerts of my life. Some of the greatest guitarists of all time shared the stage, bringing blues music to life in front of a packed audience. It was an epic night. If you ever get the chance to attend one of these shows, I highly recommend it.

One of the most powerful aspects of blues music is the storytelling. A blues singer transports you to a moment in time when they faced adversity. Many blues songs tell stories of lost love, bad luck, or hardships. A great blues song that comes to mind is "Born Under a Bad Sign," performed by Albert King. It's an incredible song—if you're having a rough day, play it, and you just might feel a little better.

Some people live their lives in a constant state of the blues. And while you *can* live that way, guess what? You'll *always* be stuck in the blues. But when you see others succeed, achieve their goals, and push past obstacles, you should feel inspired to pursue your own success and break out of the habit of living in negativity. Decide to change. Be intentional and say to yourself, "I want to be successful too, and I'm willing to do whatever it takes to get there."

Be honest with yourself about the behaviors, attitudes, and limiting beliefs holding you back from being the leader and person you want to be. Focus on fixing one or two issues at a time until you've eliminated most, if not all, of the personal challenges standing in your way. Some behaviors or limiting beliefs may take longer to change than others, so I recommend starting with your attitude. Adopting a positive attitude can help you overcome personal challenges faster and put you on the path to realizing your full potential as a leader.

One way to break free from the blues when facing personal challenges is to study how others have overcome similar struggles. Ask yourself: What challenges were they trying to overcome? How are their challenges similar to mine? What steps did they take to overcome these challenges? What resources did they use? When answering these questions, focus on the parallels between your situation and theirs. There may be differences in circumstances, but identifying the similarities will help you find the steps that might benefit you.

We're all different, and we're all driven by different things. Again, going back to the playlist analogy—if you compare your playlist to someone else's, they're probably completely different. And that's okay.

They are listening to a different tune. They have a different sound-track. They have a different voice in their head, music, or something else that drives them. To overcome your challenges, you must first look inter-nally and draw from your own experiences, knowledge, resources, and support system. This helps you create your own identity and leadership style while ensuring that the solutions you choose to overcome your chal-lenges are sustainable. These choices become a part of who you are as a person.

Finding your own solutions to the challenges you face also helps you become less vulnerable as a leader. Being comfortable admitting you're not perfect and constantly seeking ways to overcome your personal chal-lenges allows you to be more open with others and willing to discuss issues that once made you uncomfortable. It also enables you to recognize personal challenges in your team members, giving you an opportunity to help them overcome their obstacles. One of your goals as a leader is to help each member of your team succeed. Their success contributes to your success and the overall success of your organization.

Another point is that sometimes we feel embarrassed by our personal challenges, and that's normal. Once you admit there are areas where you can improve, the reaction you receive is often much different from what you expected. In fact, for some people, the *fear* of that reaction is what holds them back.

They worry they'll be judged in a certain way. But in reality, acknowl-edging your challenges demonstrates strength. It shows confidence in your abilities, who you are as a leader, and your commitment to growth. It's like showing someone your playlist and being ready to defend every song on there. *Bring it.* You're not embarrassed by any of it because that playlist reflects who you are—and, in some cases, who you aspire to be. You own who you are, and you use that to fuel the person you want to become and the direction you want to go.

Owning your differences makes you unique as a leader and, in many cases, is why people like you or want to follow you. However, being authentic and owning who you are won't always make you popular with everyone. Leaders don't need to be *liked*—they need to be *respected*. I didn't like every leader I worked with over the years, but I respected some of them. Your goal should be to develop and earn that respect and trust from your team, whether they like you personally or not. They should know that you will treat them respectfully, value their abilities and contributions, and always have the team's best interests at heart. They should also know that you genuinely want everyone on your team to succeed.

That doesn't necessarily mean they'll *like* you, especially when you push them beyond their comfort zones. However, a good leader understands the capabilities of their team and is willing to challenge them to reach their full potential and achieve success. Over time, even if they didn't enjoy every moment of the process, they will see that your leadership style worked. Ultimately, *results* matter—where everyone feels a sense of accomplishment for contributing to the team's success.

Now that you've identified and owned the things holding you back, you need a plan to overcome them. You need to create a step-by-step roadmap to transform from the old you to the new you.

One of the best ways to overcome these challenges is to create clear, attainable goals. So, what steps can you take to get past that—especially if you are an overthinker, a procrastinator, or someone with a fear of failure? How can you set the kinds of goals I mentioned before? If you don't have a goal, you'll never get to where you want to be, and you'll continue to be stuck in that cycle of never feeling good enough or never accomplishing the things you want in life. You'll keep watching other people achieve things, thinking, *That should be me.* Well, it *could* be you—if you follow these steps and are intentional and disciplined in making sure you do what's necessary to get there.

The best goal framework I've seen is the SMART method, developed by George T. Doran for setting effective goals within organizations. It is well known and widely used for helping individuals and teams plan a path for achieving their objectives.

SMART stands for specific, measurable, achievable, relevant, and time-bound.

Specific: Your goals should be clear and well-defined. Using a band analogy, let's say you want to overcome your fear of playing in front of a live audience. That's a little too generic. To get more specific, you could say, "I want to overcome my fear of playing in front of 500 or more people."

Measurable: You need to track your progress and success. You can measure each step of your progress toward your goal. You could start by performing in front of ten friends in your garage. Then you do an open mic night at a local bar in front of fifty people. Then you enter a battle of the bands showcase in front of 200 people at a local high school. Finally, you continue increasing the venue or audience size until you reach your goal of 500 people. You can track your progress at each step based on the size of the audience you play for.

Achievable: Each step has to be realistic and attainable. One of the biggest reasons people fail to achieve their goals is that they set unrealistic ones. The first time they meet resistance or realize the goal is too difficult, they quit. You can't say, "I just played in front of ten friends in my garage, so next week I'm going to book a show at Madison Square Garden in New York City." That's never going to happen. Your goals should be reasonable and within reach. After playing in front of ten friends, you could say, "I'm going to perform at a bar that holds thirty people." That's an attainable goal. Make sure your goals are challenging but achievable.

Relevant: Your goals should align with your values and objectives. If you're a musician, you might say, "This goal will help me be the best band leader I can be. When my band plays bigger shows, I'll be more comfortable performing in front of a large audience, more confident in my music, and more in sync with my bandmates. We'll go out there and rock the stage."

Time-bound: Your goal should have a deadline. For example, "I want to play in front of 500 people within six months." Setting a timeline gives you a sense of urgency and accountability.

You can create a SMART goal framework for every challenge you're trying to overcome.

Exercise: *Identify three challenges currently holding you back, and then outline three steps to overcome each of them.*

Be honest with yourself. If you can't think of three, ask a friend, coworker, or family member to identify one area where they think you can improve. We *all* have blind spots. Don't assume you're perfect. Trust me—you're not. Just ask your friends, coworkers, or significant other. If they're being honest, they'll come up with three challenges *very* quickly.

You'd be surprised how many friends and family members will openly tell you about the problems you have—problems you may not even realize yourself. They can be a great sounding board, but they're also a valuable support system to help you overcome challenges. Those close to you generally recognize that you are willing to identify areas for improvement and that you are motivated to change. If you succeed, you'll become a better friend, a better person, and someone they can collectively celebrate with. Achieving your goals with the people who matter in your life makes the journey even more rewarding.

Also, be open to criticism and feedback. We all need to be. You must be willing to take criticism, acknowledge what you know, and accept what you don't. In a previous chapter, we discussed the importance of not being defensive. To truly improve, you must embrace feedback because it helps you grow.

None of it is malicious. None of it is meant to paint you as a bad person, imply that you're not smart, or suggest that you're incompetent. It's simply about saying, "This is where I am today, and this is where I want to be."

Look at the greatest athletes of all time—what do they all have in common? Coaches. They all have people around them helping them get better.

Singers have vocal coaches to improve their technique. Performers have choreographers to enhance their stage presence. There are always people willing to help you improve because no one excels at *everything,* and no one ever will. But once you've unlocked the behaviors, attitudes, and limiting beliefs holding you back, you've removed the barriers between you and your vision.

Now, you've opened the door to becoming the leader you aspire to be. You've taken off the weights that were holding you down, and you're surrounding yourself with people who will cheer you on, motivate you, and celebrate your success because they *want* to see you become the best version of yourself.

Exercise: *List five songs that will always pull you out of the blues.*

As you work through your challenges, pursue personal growth, and work through your SMART goals, a playlist can help you stay motivated. When you're having a tough day or feel like you're struggling, have these songs ready to lift you up, inspire you, and push you forward toward your goals.

Hopefully, you'll be able to go from *blues* to *rock*—and become the best leader, teammate, and bandmate you can be.

In the next chapter, we'll begin to think boldly about your vision as a leader and establishing core principles to align your team. Ensuring your team is engaged and aligned is critical for success. We also explore defining roles on your team that support your vision for success.

PART III
PILLAR THREE: ASSEMBLING A BAND

5

ANATOMY OF A BAND

One of the most important things to do when forming a band is to determine what kind of band you want to be. What is your vision? What does success look like? Do you want to be a regular act at a local bar, or do you want to play stadiums around the world? How will you get there?

You need to set guidelines for the band to ensure everyone is on the same page. What is the band's ultimate goal? Who is your audience? Who are you playing for? And most importantly, what does each member want to get out of the band? Answering these questions establishes the band's mission.

What are your band's primary goals and objectives? Do you want to be a rock band, a country band, a metal band, or a cover band? Maybe you want to write your own music and focus on original songs. Usually, when you start a band—just like when you start a company or team—you have a mission in mind for what you want to be and what you want to accomplish. It's critical to establish that vision in music, just as it is in business.

You need to understand what type of company you have—whether software, manufacturing, or service. What are you trying to achieve? What are your goals for your team? You should clearly define your mission and how it represents the company's ultimate goal. It's also important to ensure that your mission is built to stand the test of time. Your mission should be clear and enduring, defining what the company expects to accomplish throughout its entire life cycle. Your mission serves as the inspiration for achieving the company's goals and growth.

You also need to establish values. Values are just as important in a band as they are in a company. They represent the fundamental beliefs and guiding principles for your group. So, what do you believe in? What do you value? What do you expect from each other? Examples include integrity, respect, strength, and accountability. Values are an essential part of society. We should all have them—as a country, a community, a family, or an individual.

Our values shape who we are and how we interact with others. That's why it's essential to clearly define and understand them. As a band, every member should agree on their values. Most importantly, everyone needs to buy into those values. For example, an important value for a band might be "No ego." Everyone contributes to the band's success, and you work together to accomplish your goals.

If you look at some of the greatest band leaders of all time, you'll notice that while many have confidence, some even have *swagger*. They know they're great, and they carry themselves as such. But in many cases, ego can be a major hindrance to progress, communication, and bonding as a group. We've seen countless instances where the lead singer of a popular band ends up leaving for a solo career. In some cases, ego plays a big role in their decision to leave—they believe they're bigger than the rest of the band. In other cases, the record label may influence them, saying, "You're the star here, not your bandmates. We can make you a solo star— you don't need them."

From my own experience in bands, I know that ego can be a major issue. It can make or break a band's chemistry and, ultimately, its success. Sometimes, people have an ego not necessarily because they believe they're better than everyone else but because they see themselves as the star of the band. In some cases, this mindset can erode the trust within the band.

When one person starts thinking they're more important than the rest, it can lead to a breakdown in teamwork. They might believe they can leave and start their own band, but where does that leave the rest of the team? When the ego reaches that level, it can be incredibly damaging. That's why it's critical to establish a shared set of values that everyone buys into so that ego doesn't disrupt the band's chemistry. The Rolling Stones is a great example of a band that has stood the test of time while maintaining strong group dynamics.

"No ego" is just one example of a value that can have a lasting impact on a band, but many others—communication, respect, accountability—are equally important.

Another thing to be mindful of when defining values is not simply copying someone else's. It's easy to look up the values of other successful companies or bands and adopt them because you want to emulate their success. But do those values truly reflect your company or your team? Are you being authentic in adopting someone else's values?

Who are you *really* as a company or a team? What are the guiding principles for what you're trying to achieve in your industry, with your product, or as a band? Your values may not be the same as those of another company or group you admire, and that's okay. It's always better to define your *own* identity rather than simply follow what someone else is doing. It's important to be true to yourself. Take the time to determine what your values are. They will serve as the foundation that resonates throughout your entire organization—not just for your current team members but for those you bring on board in the future.

Purpose is also essential. What impact is your team or band making in the world? If you're a band, how are you bringing people together through music? This has become increasingly important over the years, as people want to feel part of something meaningful. It's not just about making music together—it's about changing lives, influencing perspectives, and shaping how people see the world through your music.

One example that resonates with me, as I've mentioned several times in this book, is U2. I'll never forget how some of their early music inspired me—not just because of how great it sounded but because of the meaning behind their lyrics. They shed light on history and culture while highlighting struggles in their country and around the world. One song that stands out is "Pride (In the Name of Love)," which references Martin

Luther King Jr. That song, and many of their other hits, has always resonated with me. U2's purpose is evident in their lyrics and music—they genuinely seem to want to make the world a better place through what they create.

Of course, U2 is just one example. Many other bands and artists have taken a similar approach in using their music to inspire, inform, and create change.

Having purpose in the workplace is also very important. You want your people to come to work every day feeling that they're making a difference. Functioning as a cog in the wheel or making the company money without leaving a legacy or doing something meaningful isn't inspiring. It's crucial for companies to take the time to understand their purpose, gather feedback, and get input from the team on what the collective purpose should be. You want to establish a mission and values that will resonate with your team and customers and serve as a guiding light for the company for years to come.

What happens if an organization *doesn't* have a mission, values, or purpose—or maybe it has, but it doesn't communicate them regularly enough for employees to understand or even remember them?

Employee engagement suffers when a company lacks any of these core principles or fails to communicate them effectively to the team. Research supports this. According to Gallup, only 23% of U.S. employees strongly agree that they can apply their organization's values at work. According to an article on LinkedIn, a Deloitte survey found that only 21% of employees can correctly identify their company's mission statement. McKinsey & Company found that 70% of employees say their sense of purpose is defined by their work—meaning where they work and what they do directly shapes their sense of purpose.

Additionally, Gallup reports that companies with a highly engaged workforce enjoy a 21% increase in profitability. This means companies that fail to effectively align their team with their mission, values, and purpose could lose up to 21% in potential profits. If you're a company generating $100 million a year, that's a potential $21 million loss in profitability simply due to a lack of employee engagement.

To help companies bridge this gap, I've created a workshop focused on boosting employee engagement in these areas. The workshop aims to help teams develop a deep and practical understanding of their company's mission, values, and purpose by creating a song that reflects these principles. It's an excellent team-building exercise because it allows everyone to share how the company's mission, values, and purpose impact their specific roles and how they align with the company's broader goals and objectives. If you're interested in learning more, visit my website: www.mattertree.com.

Music is a powerful mnemonic device for this exercise because it helps us remember things. Remember our discussion on commercial jingles, TV themes, and movie soundtracks? Remember when I said I couldn't get the *Schoolhouse Rock* video "I'm Just a Bill" out of my head? Imagine if your team could recall your company's mission, values, and purpose quickly and clearly by remembering a song they helped create. This would improve employee engagement, and as research shows, it could also significantly boost your company's profits.

The goal is to ensure your core principles are something that everyone buys into—something clear, easy to understand, and, most importantly, something they can *live by* on a daily basis. Once you establish the company's core principles, you must continuously communicate them to your team. It's not something you define once and then set aside.

You should revisit it regularly to ensure that, as your company grows, everyone continues to buy into it collectively. Once you've established your guidelines—your mission, values, and purpose—the next step is to identify the roles needed to accomplish its goals. You need to assemble a team that reflects these core principles in order to be successful.

For example, if your primary goal is to be a successful country band, you need to add specific roles that align with that genre. You'll likely include a drummer, a bass player, one or more guitar players (including a pedal steel or lap steel guitar player), a lead singer, and possibly a fiddle player. These roles are determined by what is needed to achieve the goals and objectives of your band's mission.

At the same time, you want to ensure that the band's structure supports the purpose you've outlined. If your goal is to be a jazz band, the lineup might look different from that of a country band. You might include a drummer, an upright bass player, a guitarist, a horn section, and a pianist, with no lead singer if you prefer an instrumental band.

Of course, many great jazz singers have made a lasting impact on music, but again, the roles and structure of your organization should reflect your mission, the sound you want to create, and what you aim to achieve. I think of bands like Earth, Wind & Fire, one of my all-time favorites. They had a large ensemble of instrumentalists on stage, each with a distinct purpose. They had a horn section, a drummer, a percussionist, an incredible bass player, several great singers, a guitarist, a keyboardist—they had it all. That was the sound they envisioned, and they successfully brought it to life. They've had several major hits over the years, and their music continues to be a part of our daily lives because of its energy and positivity. I hear Earth, Wind & Fire songs almost every week, and it's inspiring that their mission to create uplifting and positive music has stood the test of time.

The roles and instrumentalists you add to your band are also crucial. You want musicians who play their instruments well and align with the mission, values, and purpose you've set forth. When defining roles that support your vision, you need to understand how each position contributes to that vision. As I mentioned earlier, whether you're forming a jazz band or a country band, the musicians must be talented and highly skilled in their specific genre. If you're hiring a drummer for a jazz band, you need a drummer who specializes in jazz. Likewise, your guitarist should be a jazz guitarist. You wouldn't put a metal guitarist in a jazz band —it simply wouldn't work.

I've been in bands where we brought in classically trained musicians who weren't well-suited to playing rock, R&B, or alternative music. It was evident that the fit wasn't right—their playing didn't match the band's style.

The same principle applies in business.

If you run an accounting software-as-a-service (SaaS) company, you'll want to ensure that your leadership team has experience in that space. You want to hire individuals who are adept in accounting, particularly in as many key roles as possible on your team. For example, you'd want to ensure that your attorney has experience with SaaS agreements and understands the legal regulations and applicable laws specific to that type of company. You also want to ensure that your CTO has experience with SaaS-related products, understands how to develop them, and knows how to build and maintain a skilled team of programmers. They should be capable of overseeing IT operations, maintaining the underlying software, and developing new products that expand beyond the core offering.

Hiring professionals with familiarity in your industry ensures that everyone is aligned, working toward the same goals, and adhering to the established mission, values, and purpose. This cohesion allows the team to function like a well-rehearsed band, where each member understands and performs their role seamlessly.

In some cases, you may hire people who don't have direct experience in accounting, for example (referring back to the accounting SaaS company example), but who have strengths in other areas. They can develop the skills necessary to thrive in their roles with the right support and training.

> **Exercise:** *If your team were a band, what instrument would each team member play and why? Additionally, what song would your band play that best reflects the personality of the group?*

This is a fun exercise. Returning to the accounting SaaS company example, your lawyer might be the bass player because they lay down the foundational protections for the company, ensuring compliance with laws and regulations and maintaining the company's legal stability. Your lead guitar player might be your CTO, driving innovation and pushing boundaries—each guitar solo representing a new and creative way to improve the product. Your CEO might be the lead singer, as they are the face of the company and lead the team toward its vision.

These are just examples of how different roles can metaphorically fit into the structure of a band. Have fun determining how each person's personality and skill set contribute to your organization's dynamics.

> **Exercise:** *If you were in a real band, what instrument would you want to play? More importantly, what instrument do you feel truly reflects your personality, values, mission, and purpose?*

Consider where you would best fit within the band dynamic.

In the next chapter, we'll look at finding the right people to fill the roles you've established for your team. This is critical to ensure your team performs and consistently executes at a high level. It's also important for building team chemistry and creating a healthy culture.

6

FINDING THE RIGHT FIT

*N*ow that you've established your mission, values, and purpose and know your band's (or company's) mission, you have a clear direction.

You've defined the values and principles that your employees—or bandmates—will align with, such as respect, communication, and accountability. You understand your purpose: how you plan to make an impact by changing the world or simply making it a better place through your work. You've also identified the roles you need.

You know what kind of company you are, just as a band knows what kind of music it plays. You're now building your team based on your core values, mission, and the roles and responsibilities required to accomplish your organization's goals and realize its vision.

So now you have to define who your ideal bandmates might be. Think of it this way: your team is your band. You want to find the type of person who would be a great fit for that role. I've been in bands with different skill levels, commitment, and interest, and they rarely worked. You can tell when band members aren't practicing their parts or when you play a song together and it just doesn't sound right. In hindsight, they didn't align with the goals and objectives of the band because they weren't on the same page. They had a different timeline and agenda than what the band was trying to accomplish collectively.

Some employees may not be aligned with your company's mission, values, and purpose. That can disrupt progress and act as a headwind, preventing you from reaching your organization's ultimate goals and objectives. If you're in a cover band that wants to play out at least two weekends a month, you need to find bandmates with the time to practice and are available to play on those weekends.

I've been in bands where the singer would show up late, or the drummer had other commitments that took priority. They weren't truly dedicated to what we were trying to achieve as a band. They just weren't putting in the time. They weren't practicing. They weren't showing up to shows when they should. You could tell their level of energy and interest was completely different from the other members of the band. I've also been in multiple bands where each of us had differing levels of commitment and perspective on the band's potential.

Conversely, I've been in bands where I knew we weren't as good as some of the other members thought we were. In those cases, it affected my level of commitment. I often tried to leave the band because I didn't want to hold them back by not being all in. That lack of commitment could have hurt what they were trying to accomplish as a group. This is why it's crucial to identify differences in personality, fit, and commitment when bringing someone onto your team.

Sometimes, the best fit for your band isn't necessarily the person with the best technical skills but rather someone with the commitment and intangibles that make them the right choice.

I am primarily a guitar player, but when I was younger, I would join any band that would take me, and I was willing to play any instrument I could just to be part of the band. There were times I joined as a bass player simply to be included. I wasn't the best bass player, but I learned the songs, showed up to practice on time, and played well enough for the band to sound good. I was also a decent vocalist, so I could sing lead on some songs and backup on others.

I brought energy, and I felt the chemistry in the group was so strong that we could go out, play live, and make it work—even without me being the best bass player. Ultimately, the role I played was a perfect fit for that particular band at that time. Again, you want to make sure that you bring in people who are a good fit—not just in skill but in dedication and chemistry as well.

So how do you find people you think will be the right fit for the roles you've identified? This is a big challenge for companies, which is why many use third-party search platforms or recruiters to find candidates. That's certainly one approach—you can solicit resumes and search for people outside your network. But I always say the best way, at least when I was in a band, to fill a role was to ask someone in the band if they knew anyone. "Hey, do you know a drummer?" And the bass player might raise his hand and say, "Oh yeah, I know this guy. I'll bring him in to audition." And now you're jamming with this new guy to see if he's the right fit.

That happens all the time in bands, and it works really well because you're bringing in someone who already has a connection to a member of the band. Your bandmates already understand the mission, values, and purpose of the group and can recommend someone they feel is the right fit. They also have a vested interest in making a good choice because they know they'll be blamed if it doesn't work out.

So they would know whether the new drummer you're bringing in fits those values, mission, and purpose. If they don't, they likely wouldn't recommend them, even if they're a great drummer, because they still may not be the right fit for your particular band. That's why I always say the best place to start is with people in your band.

In some cases, you might know of a good potential fit, but may not know them personally. Maybe, you've seen them play in another band. I've been to shows where I saw drummers on stage that blew me away, and I thought, *Wow, that drummer would be perfect for my band.* The same applies in business. You might attend conferences, hear people speak, interact with them, or even negotiate with someone on the other side of a deal.

As an attorney, I've had several situations where I was negotiating with someone from another company and was so impressed by how smart they were and what a great attorney they were that I thought, *This person would be a great fit for our organization.* We're constantly meeting people and running into potential candidates who could be a good fit for our band or company based on our experiences with them.

If no one in the band can make a personal recommendation for a drummer, the next step is to reach out to people you know and trust and ask if they know someone. Maybe band members can seek referrals from friends who understand the position you're trying to fill and the qualities you're looking for. That would be another solid option for finding the right fit for your organization.

Of course, you could also take out an ad in a newspaper. There's a story about the band Kiss—back in December 1972, they posted an ad in *The Village Voice* in New York looking for a guitar player with "flash and ability." And guess who answered the ad? Ace Frehley, who went on to become an amazing guitarist for the band and was crucial to their success. Sometimes, placing an ad works. It helps when you know what you're looking for—in this case, someone with flash and ability. Those were the qualities they were looking for in a bandmate, and they found them in their new guitarist.

A company needs to know what they're looking for beyond skills and experience. Seek out those qualities in the people you interview and bring on, especially if you don't have any prior connection with them. These qualities might include being punctual, prepared, self-motivated, and a team player, or having a positive attitude, a relentless work ethic, and a drive for innovation. Take the time to determine what qualities you need for the roles you are looking to fill. In some cases, "flash and ability" might be enough.

I've had roles where I needed to hire people, and oftentimes, I didn't hire the person with the best resume or the most relevant skills. I often look for the person I think would be the best fit for the organization. Whether it's a band or a company, I focus on how they might grow within the group and the impact they could have. Sometimes, they may not have all the necessary skills upfront, but I can see that, from a chemistry standpoint, they would fill the role perfectly.

They can grow with the band and truly become part of the overall vision because they buy into the mission, values, and purpose. I've interviewed people who didn't align with those values, and if you conduct a strong interview process, you can often spot potential red flags that indicate they are not fully aligned with your organization's core principles.

Do your best to identify any potential issues with a candidate regarding skills, team fit, chemistry, and alignment with your company's core principles during the hiring process. This will save you time, money, and frustration down the road. You won't always get it right, but you should take the time to understand why a particular candidate didn't work out and use that information to improve your hiring process. The goal is to continuously refine your approach to increase the number of successful hires who turn out to be a great fit for your organization. This is why it's so important to adhere to your mission, values, and purpose when interviewing candidates.

Sometimes, we make hiring decisions for the wrong reasons. One reason is urgency—when there's an immediate need to fill a role, we may hire someone simply based on their resume or what an AI filtering system suggests. Nowadays, many resumes go through an automated screening process before they even reach a hiring manager's desk. A candidate might align skill-wise or have the right experience on paper, but are they truly the right fit for what your company is trying to achieve?

This is where many companies make hiring mistakes. They focus only on finding someone with the right experience to hit the ground running rather than ensuring the candidate aligns with the company's mission, values, and purpose. Many people have experienced hiring someone they initially thought was a good fit, only to realize later they weren't. In hindsight, companies often recognize that they failed to assess alignment with their core principles during the interview process. The key question becomes: Is there a better way to uncover that fit before hiring?

One solution is to be intentional with the questions you ask.

As a group, take the time to develop thoughtful questions that will reveal whether a candidate truly aligns with your organization. Too often, I've seen companies conduct interviews without clear guidelines for the interviewers. Candidates come in, and the interviewer, busy with other tasks, quickly skims the resume at the last minute and asks a few generic questions about experience and why they want the job.

Explain your experience here. Why do you want to join our company?

How do you think you can add value? Where do you see yourself in five years? These are the standard interview questions we've all probably heard or even asked ourselves. But do those questions truly uncover whether a person is a good fit for your organization? You have to be intentional about asking the right questions during the interview process.

Everyone on the interview team should understand the specific questions they need to ask to find the right fit for your company. Most importantly, they should also understand what kind of answers to look for to ensure the candidate aligns with the company's goals, objectives, mission, values, and purpose.

Some companies use assessments to weed out potential candidates, but there is no substitute for looking someone in the eye, asking a question, and seeing their response. How long did it take them to answer? Were they long-winded or concise? Did they make eye contact? Were they confident in their response? Did they smile? What was their attitude? Did you notice any nervous habits (playing with hair, hand gestures, rapid blinking)? Were they articulate? And most importantly, did they actually answer your question? You also want them to ask questions about the company, the job, the culture, and the leadership to determine if it's the right fit for them.

But even with a keen eye and ear, you're not always going to be 100% right. You will hire people who just aren't the right fit. Unfortunately, that's the reality of hiring. In some cases, candidates perform well on assessments and say all the right things in the interview, but once they start working with your team, you realize that their behavior or work style doesn't align with what they said in their interview.

However, even in these cases, there's still an opportunity to align them with your mission, values, and purpose. By emphasizing these principles from day one, you set clear expectations. Then, through the leadership principles discussed in this book, you work to ensure they buy into the company culture, work in harmony with the team, and build chemistry within the organization.

One option is to create a professional development plan that helps them see a path for success within your company. Find out what they want to do, where they want to grow, and how they want to develop. This can help identify ways they can best contribute to your organization. You should want everyone in your company to succeed, and as a leader, you should facilitate that success. Ensure they are in the right role. If they could be more valuable in another part of the organization, explore that option. Ensure they optimize their potential and provide them with the necessary resources to thrive and be their best.

You want someone who will adhere to your core principles, collaborate well with the team, help inspire and motivate others, and contribute creative and innovative ideas.

All of this is essential to ensuring they grow with the team and help accomplish the goals and objectives set for your band or company. But what if someone doesn't fit into the company culture? What if you bring someone in, thinking they are the right fit because they have the skills, a strong referral, or prior experience you admire, only to realize later that they don't truly align with the team?

The reality is that you don't truly know people until you spend time working with them. Over time, you learn about their personality, quirks, temperament, and work ethic. Maybe after working with them for a while, you realize they're not the right fit. In that case, there are a few ways to approach the situation.

One option is to coach them by giving them guidelines on company culture and creating a game plan to help them acclimate to the group. This is where communication is critical. Ask questions like, "What can we do to help you be more successful in your role?" or "What challenges are you facing as you work to achieve your goals?" Then, listen to their feedback. It will often surprise you. It might be something simple. They might say, "I don't know what other groups are doing," or "I'm not sure how my role fits into the bigger picture," or even "I don't understand why my work is important." As a leader, you can address those concerns. You can explain why they are a critical piece of the puzzle that is the organization's success. You coach them. You provide clear expectations. You identify pain points in the relationship and work together to address them. Then, you set goals.

Another option is to assign a mentor—someone else in the group who can guide them, help them fit in, and answer their questions. A mentor can also help them better understand the culture, the chemistry, and why everyone has bought into the team's goals and objectives.

Encourage them to be part of the success. In your conversations, ask, "What do you want to do? Where do you see yourself growing in the organization? How do you see yourself adding the most value to the team?" Hopefully, their answers will help create a clear path to success.

Another question to ask is, "What else can we do to help you succeed here?" Because when they succeed, it benefits you as a leader, strengthens your team, and, most importantly, helps the company thrive. Imagine if most or all of your team members were operating at their full potential and succeeding in their roles. Now the band is rocking! Everyone's in tune, on beat, and jamming their hearts out. There's no stopping what you can accomplish and where you can grow—together.

This also improves retention because people on your team want to be there. It helps attract new talent, boosts communication, enhances morale, fosters collaboration, and strengthens the company culture.

At the same time, it's important to recognize when someone is not a good fit for the organization. You need to act quickly—either by helping them overcome their challenges or making the tough decision to move on. It's okay to conclude that someone isn't going to work out.

Once you determine that a person is not the right fit, I encourage you to take swift action. I've been in organizations where people clearly weren't a good fit but stayed far longer than they should have. This creates issues with company culture because disgruntled employees can have a toxic effect. When someone doesn't want to be there, their negative attitude can spread to others.

It only takes one person's frustration to bleed into the rest of the organization. They start complaining to colleagues, talking about things and people they don't like. This negativity can become very disruptive to the team. Even if most voices are positive, that one negative voice can resonate and influence others. Some employees might start questioning leadership, the organization, or their commitment to the team. It counteracts what you're trying to do as a leader—build the organization and ensure everyone sings the same tune.

It is important to remove any disruptive members and show that you are a strong leader who follows the core principles you established. Whenever there is a cultural issue in your organization, your team looks to you as a leader to do something about it. All eyes are on you. How you handle it will either strengthen or erode the level of confidence and trust your team has in you. That's why it's important to always listen to your team. Recognize when there's dysfunction and act swiftly to address it. As a leader, you will be judged not by your team's hardships and challenges but by how you respond to them.

> **Exercise:**
> 1. What are the three most important traits—the key qualities you want in a team member? What are your non-negotiables? What must they have—or not have?
> 2. What song embodies your ideal team member?

For question one: Know your non-negotiables, and craft your interview questions to assess them. If a candidate isn't willing to meet your expectations, and those expectations are non-negotiable, don't bring them on board. For example, maybe one is punctuality: they have to show up on time. If they don't, they will disappoint you, and you'll have to go through the process of removing them and finding someone else. Keeping your must-have needs in mind will help you weed through candidates.

For question two: There are a lot of great songs out there. Think about one that reflects qualities like resilience, teamwork, punctuality, or dedication—whatever it might be.

A senior executive of a global company revealed to me that one of the questions they ask candidates in interviews is, "What's your favorite album?" or "What's your favorite song?" They feel that the answer to this question reflects who that person is and whether they'd be a good fit for the organization. It ties back to what we discussed earlier about how your playlist reflects who you are. Saying the right album or song might be enough to get you hired because it resonates with someone on the hiring team. You never know what might tip the scales in your favor, and music can be a great way to establish connections.

> **Exercise:** *Who is your favorite band member of all time, and why?*

We all have different bands we love, but a particular member usually stands out to us.

I talked about Van Halen earlier in this book. I grew up listening to Eddie. As a guitar player, I watched what Eddie was doing. He was my favorite bandmate in Van Halen because of his incredible guitar playing. However, some people may say David Lee Roth was their favorite member of Van Halen.

There are so many other bands where you can pick a favorite member. It might be James Hetfield of Metallica, Amy Lee of Evanescence, Q-Tip of A Tribe Called Quest, Jimmy Page of Led Zeppelin, Jack White of The White Stripes, Stephen Malkmus of Pavement, or someone else. It's a fun exercise to think about who your favorite band member is and why.

Reflect on it. Why did you pick that person? What characteristics do you admire? What traits do they have that resonate with you? Do you see any of those traits in yourself? Maybe you can adopt some of those traits to become a better leader and person.

In the next chapter, we'll dive into the importance of getting to know your team—from finding personal and professional commonalities to finding opportunities to collaborate. The more you work together, the better you know your team. This helps leaders get a better understanding of team strengths and weaknesses, and lays the groundwork for improvement.

PART IV
PILLAR FOUR: PRACTICE, PRACTICE, PRACTICE

7

JAM SESSIONS

The only way to get good at anything is to practice. If you want to improve as a band, you need to practice together—whether you're rehearsing songs for recording or preparing for a live performance. The same principle applies to business.

Whether you're an accountant, marketing executive, attorney, or chief technology officer, consistently learning, growing, and applying what you've learned helps you progress in your role. A great example of this is the use of the word "practice" to describe medical groups or law offices. Professionals in those fields are expected to develop their skills continuously through education and experience. While the standards might be different, the same applies in business—where growth happens both individually and as a team.

You need to collaborate as a team or, using a musical analogy, "jam" together. The goal is to develop chemistry through effective collaboration. This could mean a leadership team learning to run a business together, developing innovative products, or creating marketing campaigns that resonate with customers. Any group effort in your organization can be considered "practice"—a way to understand each other professionally and personally and to learn and grow from mistakes.

"Understanding each other" can mean finding professional and personal commonalities to bond with your teammates. The goal is to figure out how to create the best "music" together. How can you bring out the best in each other to create something special? How can you stay committed and present with your team to achieve a common goal? How can you take advantage of opportunities to collaborate on projects, professional development, charitable endeavors, and other initiatives? These are just a few ways to consistently seek opportunities to "jam" together. In turn, you learn more about each other, recognize the team's strengths, and engage in honesty about both strengths and potential weaknesses.

The only way to uncover this is through practice. Using my musical analogy, imagine you've put your band together. You've defined your mission, values, purpose, and objectives. You know what kind of band you want to be. You've identified the roles you need in your band. Everyone is there, with their instruments tuned and ready to go.

You've assembled a great group of musicians, and now curiosity sets in —how will we sound together? You never know; you might not sound great at first, even though you've gone through the painstaking process of selecting the best people. You've identified the ideal bandmates based on their roles and how they fit into the bigger picture, but chances are, it won't sound perfect at your first practice.

The reason is that you don't really know each other's tendencies. You don't know each other's skills. You don't know each other's timing. You don't know what the other person is going to do. You haven't yet established any chemistry within the group. The only way to do that is by jamming together.

One of the best moments I've ever had as a musician—and I'm sure other musicians can attest to this—is when you're with a group of people, playing your first song together. You start grooving. You start feeling like, *Wow, this is sounding really good.*

As you play together, the band members open up and show their personalities. You might be the guitar player, and when you hear that drum fill, you play off of that. Maybe you add a little riff on the guitar, and the bass player adds a little run on the bass. Now you guys are starting to vibe, you're starting to groove, and you're beginning to learn what each person can do, feeding off each other.

Let's say the singer suddenly starts belting out a song while the band is playing. The singer is on point, and the song is great. Maybe she's coming up with some fantastic ideas, or maybe you're doing a cover song, and she's nailing the vocals—not just singing the lyrics but conveying the emotion behind them. What she's feeling is essentially the energy from the band coming through her, completing the song.

And the more you jam together as a band, the better you get. When I was in cover bands, we weren't very good at first because we were just learning the songs. It starts with each member learning their part. Once you know your part, you come together, practice, and jam to see if all the individual parts work well together to create an amazing song. A lot of times, it takes time to get there. The timing may be off. Maybe the way one person learned the song differs slightly from how another band member learned it.

The only way to overcome that is through practice—constant practice. You have to feed off each other, listen to what the other band members are playing, and adapt. You may try to add a fill or a little flourish to make the song your own. That's what creates the magic and brings the music to life.

It's the same thing in business. As I said, you should take advantage of opportunities to collaborate in the workplace—whether through meetings, projects, charitable causes, or even grabbing lunch together. Any chance you have to bond and gel—professionally or personally—take it. You should also consider meeting outside of work for team-building sessions, like workshops or retreats. This is an opportunity to get out of the office environment and connect with people on a personal level while also getting to know them better professionally. It allows you to build the chemistry I'm talking about. As a leader, you should take the time to get to know your team.

The better you know your team, the better you will be at resolving conflicts, which are inevitable. Every organization experiences conflict;

what matters is how you respond to it. If your team has chemistry and is aligned with the company's core principles, they may be able to take the lead themselves to resolve their issues. This would be the ideal scenario—where you empower your team members to work through conflicts together.

For example, if a conflict arises over the direction of a project two team members are working on, encourage them to ask questions about which direction best aligns with the company's mission, values, and purpose. If they still need help resolving their differences, ensure that clear communication channels are in place so they can reach you or another leader for a quick resolution. Remember, time is of the essence, especially in business. You want to make sure you resolve any conflicts quickly and decisively.

Your biggest asset is your people—the individuals you hire or work with to achieve the company's goals and objectives. It's not the products, the buildings, or the equipment you own. It truly is your people. Because of this, you should invest time in helping them grow within your organization. Ask them questions and engage with them regularly to understand their aspirations and how they want to succeed in your company.

Employees view their positions in one of two ways: as a job or as a career. If it's just a job, then your company is merely a stepping stone. But if it's a career, it's a place where they see opportunities to grow and become leaders within your organization.

As a leader, you want people on your team who aspire to build a career with your company. That means they will grow with the organization, play a role in succession planning, and help generate new revenue by attracting customers and contributing creative ideas to improve products. There are countless ways employees can help propel a company forward.

Their success translates to your success. The more you inspire and motivate your team as a leader, the better your company will be. That's why it's essential to ensure your employees succeed in their roles. They can drive company growth, productivity, creativity, and innovation. They can generate ideas that improve your products and make your organization more efficient from an operational standpoint. You will build an outstanding company if you hire the best people and maximize their personal skills and growth.

Focusing on the success of each team member also improves retention. It attracts top talent who want to work in a company with a culture that supports their individual growth. It enhances communication within the organization. It boosts morale because everyone is aligned, working in sync, and moving toward a common goal. When you assemble a great team, and they function like a choir—singing in rhythm, tempo, and harmony—your organization will continue to thrive for years to come. This will not only encourage employees to follow your leadership and stay with the company, but it will also strengthen your business and help you achieve your goals and objectives.

What I've found to be very important in business is when a leader takes an interest in employees. As a leader, you're busy running the company, with a million things on your plate, but if you can take just five minutes to check in with an employee, it can make all the difference. It's important to create moments to engage with your employees, preferably one-on-one. This may not always be practical in larger companies, but you can still achieve this through group sessions. As a leader, you might invite ten employees to get together and talk about the business and their aspirations. Maybe you go to lunch or create another opportunity to engage, share ideas, and exchange feedback. These interactions help build the team chemistry I'm talking about.

One of the best ways to foster that connection is through storytelling. Let's say there's a new associate employee at your company. At first, they're trying to learn the company culture and adjust to their new responsibilities. They're diving into the work you've given them, and inevitably, challenges arise. They'll have a lot of questions, and they want to make sure they're doing things the right way, following the company's processes—which may be different from what they're used to.

Every new job comes with growing pains. Everyone wants to know if they're doing a good job, but unless someone tells them, they're left guessing. Based on their experience, they may gauge their performance without direct feedback. But what I've found to be the most powerful way to ease that uncertainty for employees is when you step in as a leader. You can tell them what they're doing well to boost their confidence and also share a story about your own experiences. That kind of reassurance can help put their mind at ease and motivate them to keep going. Stories are a powerful way to engage employees and make them feel more connected to you and the company.

You might say, "When I first joined this company, I had no idea what I was doing. I struggled for months trying to fit in. These are the things I did to improve." You can also channel something a previous boss did or said to help you overcome challenges and share that with your employees.

Stories like these are powerful for several reasons. First, they let employees know, "Wow, he or she was just like me. They went through the same struggles I'm experiencing. And not only did they succeed, but they are now leading the company." That kind of reassurance can be incredibly motivating. It helps employees see that if their boss faced similar struggles and overcame them, they can too. That's much more powerful than simply saying, "Here are three things you need to do to improve."

Storytelling also adds a personal touch. I see it as a way to build a personal bond with employees, creating a deeper level of engagement and trust. Even in a professional setting, sharing personal stories that others can relate to helps them see that they're not alone. They recognize that others have faced similar struggles and that there is someone they can lean on or talk to for guidance. Anytime a leader has the opportunity to use storytelling as a way to engage, inspire, and motivate their team, they should absolutely do it. Tell as many stories as possible because that resonates most with the people you're trying to connect with.

Often, employees will take those stories and add their own, sharing them with others who come up behind them. One of my most impactful moments was when I was a young attorney at a big law firm, participating in a negotiation workshop. In this workshop, they paired senior attorneys with younger attorneys. I was fortunate to be paired with the founding partner of the law firm. It's something I still talk about to this day—being a young associate, trying to find my way and understand my place in the firm, and suddenly finding myself face-to-face with the founding partner.

I had quality time with him, where I could ask him questions directly, with no one else around. He mentored me, shared stories, answered my questions, and provided the kind of reassurance that storytelling can offer. That moment has stayed with me throughout my entire career. It probably didn't mean much to him—he was likely paired with young attorneys all the time, and it might have felt like just another workshop. But to me, it meant the world. And that's what matters.

After that experience, I felt more connected to the firm than ever before. It was a life-changing professional opportunity to engage with him. His reassurances made me feel like I truly belonged there. The way we worked together through that workshop solidified my confidence in my role at the firm. That's why, as a leader, it's so important to instill those principles—or at least use them as a guiding light—to help employees feel more engaged, inspired, motivated, and reassured that they are valuable members of the team, contributing to the organization's growth and success.

The second moment that stands out, and another reason why I wrote this book, relates to music. I was working with a Fortune 200 client when I started talking with one of the senior executives about music. We came from completely different backgrounds—geographically, culturally, and professionally. I don't even remember how the topic came up, but I mentioned the show *Live From Daryl's House*, created by Daryl Hall of Hall & Oates. I brought up my favorite episode, featuring The O'Jays—one of my favorite groups of all time. I love The O'Jays. Instantly, we bonded over that show and that group. We began sharing stories about their music and other artists we liked. That connection over music immediately made me feel like part of the team and strengthened our working relationship. Even after my consultancy ended with that client, I stayed in touch with the senior executive, and we remain friends to this day. It's another example of how music is such a powerful vehicle for bringing people together. It can create connections almost instantly, perhaps more than anything else in life. That's why music is so important to us—and why companies should consider using musical principles to enhance leadership effectiveness and strengthen company culture.

As you build team chemistry, it's important to understand the strengths and weaknesses of each team member—including yourself. As a leader, you want to recognize and leverage your team's strengths to achieve your company's goals and objectives.

We all have strengths and weaknesses. Nobody's perfect; nobody can do everything. Even leaders have blind spots—every leader does. No matter how great a leader may be, there are always areas for improvement. That is 100% true for every leader out there.

This applies to your team as well. They will have strengths in certain areas and weaknesses in others. Understanding these strengths and weaknesses is essential. As you "practice" with your team, you should be proactive in identifying their strengths. What are they really good at as a team? Individually? Of course, this takes time and requires constant communication and feedback to truly understand the full potential of your team.

In the context of music, imagine your band is jamming, and you ask your guitar player to play a solo. But then, the solo doesn't blow you away. It's okay, but it's not what you were hoping for. You expected a solo that would elevate the song and inspire everyone else to raise their game.

At that point, you realize that your lead guitar player isn't as strong at improvising as you had hoped. When he practices a solo beforehand, he nails it note for note when playing live. But if you ask him to improvise on the spot, the solo is not as dynamic. In that case, he can improve with practice. Over time, he may become a great lead guitar player.

Now that you've identified a weakness in the band, you can take steps to address it. You can overcome weaknesses through learning and practice, but sometimes you may need to adjust your team structure. If you realize that your guitarist is good but not strong enough as a lead player, you can add another member to the team—someone specifically to play lead guitar.

Maybe your band is better suited with two guitar players. Many famous bands operate this way—Def Leppard and Guns N' Roses both have two guitarists. Usually, one serves as the lead guitarist, while the other focuses on rhythm, though sometimes they trade off. When you clearly identify strengths and weaknesses, you better understand your team's overall capabilities. You can pinpoint challenges, determine how to overcome them, and decide what additional pieces you may need to add to make your team—or your band—complete.

Another example is that every singer has a finite vocal range—no one can sing all octaves. Some singers have incredible ranges, but every lead singer has their limits. That's why you'll want to write songs that fit within their vocal range. If you're in a cover band, you may want a singer with a broader vocal range to cover as many songs as possible. You can also add more lead singers or background vocalists to support a wider variety of songs. However, if you're in a tribute band, your singer only needs to match the vocal range of the original artist. There are many different ways to approach it.

I talked earlier about the band Earth, Wind & Fire, which was a huge influence on me. My brother used to play their music when we were growing up, and I loved everything about the band. They had two singers: Maurice White, the lead singer, who had an incredible vocal range, and Philip Bailey, who could sing falsetto and handle the high parts. They complemented each other so well, which expanded their song range. Some songs featured Maurice White, while others featured Philip Bailey, allowing them to cover a broader range of styles. This made them an even more impactful band and led to more hits. Their music will stand the test of time on so many levels because they were such a talented group.

You should also consider that even if a band member isn't strong in one area, they may add value in others, such as songwriting, production, vocals, or stage presence. The most important aspect of team dynamics is chemistry—working well together to overcome challenges and accomplish goals. When there is chemistry, it's easier to balance the strengths and weaknesses within the team. If there is a lack of chemistry, then you need to focus on building it—whether by working with the current team members or making changes to achieve it.

The goal is not to criticize anyone but to recognize that every team member has strengths and weaknesses, whether related to skills, behavior, attitude, or limiting beliefs. The key is to understand these strengths and weaknesses and, as a leader, create a strategy that maximizes the team's performance and productivity. If you can do that, you'll give your team and organization the best chance to succeed.

Exercise:
1. List the biggest strengths and the biggest weaknesses of your team.
2. Identify three steps you can take to turn a weakness into a strength.

For exercise one: Be completely honest. If you need help preparing this list, ask your team: *What are we doing well? Where can we improve?* Regularly asking these questions will help your team continue to improve over time. Don't just ask them once—make it a habit. Consider asking every three to six months to ensure ongoing growth and development.

Evaluate your weaknesses in the context of your product, business, team, and customers. How can you improve these weaknesses? How can you turn them into strengths?

For exercise two: Be intentional and thoughtful about actions you can take to address these challenges. If you or your team can't immediately identify solutions, research how other teams have overcome similar issues and test those strategies. Continuously ask, *How can we be better? How can we overcome our weaknesses?* That's how your team will grow.

Exercise: *Identify your favorite band of all time and explain why.*

The reason for this exercise is to explore which bands have had the greatest impact on you and why. Maybe they've inspired or motivated you or helped you overcome a challenge in your life. If this band has influenced you in such a way, write down your story. Consider sharing it with someone facing a similar challenge—it might help them overcome their struggle and make a difference in their life.

In the next chapter, we'll explore how you can adapt your leadership style to optimize team performance and build team harmony by aligning individual contributions with organizational goals. Prioritizing the success of your team members gives your organization the best chance to stay in tune and in rhythm.

8

GET THE MUSIC TIGHT

*B*e intentional in how you approach improving every day.

After assessing your current leadership style and visualizing where you want it to be, you need to create a plan to get there. In my experience, planning is key to accomplishing anything in life. We've all heard this before, but how many of us actually do it? Setting SMART goals—as we discussed in Chapter 4—is the first step, but execution is what ultimately gets you to your destination.

Solicit feedback from your team and customers to ensure you're on the right track. Implement and optimize communication and feedback channels, and seek to reduce micromanagement. If you want to adapt your leadership style to optimize team performance, understanding your team—knowing what makes them tick, their strengths, and their weaknesses—is key, as discussed in the previous chapter. Now that you know these factors, you should consider adapting your leadership style to maximize your team's performance based on that information. You want to be intentional about how you approach each day.

Let's say one of your company's strengths is that you're great at meeting deadlines, but one of your weaknesses is quality control—you meet deadlines, but the quality isn't always where you want it to be. You need to examine your team and determine why that is the case. Maybe the person leading the quality control group needs additional training, or maybe they are not closely following the checklist or quality parameters you've set. Perhaps they're not planning ahead to ensure quality is a priority from the beginning of the process, instead of waiting until the middle or later stages to emphasize it.

As a leader, you need to first understand the weakness and why it's happening. Then you can address it to ensure first-rate quality control. If your team is meeting deadlines, you're accomplishing part of your goals, which is great. But if the weakness is hurting you—if you're not putting out the best-quality product possible—then what reaches your customers could damage your brand and business. If a competitor produces higher-quality products, that can hurt your market share and overall success as an organization. So if you see these issues arising, be the leader, be proactive, step up to assess the situation, and figure out where the pain points are.

It might be a personnel issue. Again, sometimes the person running that group needs more training, education, or motivation—whatever it might be. In some cases, you may need to replace that person with someone who can meet the criteria and expectations you've set for quality control. Having a plan to overcome that is very important.

You'll remember the discussion of the SMART goal process where you have a plan for improvement. You could create a six-month plan to improve quality control so that your products start to meet the standards you've set for your organization. One of the best ways to do this is by improving communication and feedback channels.

Sometimes, leaders are so busy that they don't really listen to the pulse or the rhythm of their organization. They're handling daily fire drills, constantly putting out fires, and addressing urgent matters that overwhelm them. As a result, they may lose touch with what's happening within their company culture.

Leaders can rely on their team or managers to provide them with important information. However, in some cases, that information may not reach the CEO or leader as clearly as it should. Issues can get lost in translation, especially when concerns from lower-level employees work their way up the management chain.

By the time an issue reaches the leader, it may have changed entirely—it gets distorted, and the urgency or core pain point may no longer be clear. As a leader, you are focused on higher-level issues, so you often delegate your team to handle the minutiae of the organization. The problem with this approach is that you may miss out on crucial information in the feedback loop, which could be critical to your business growth.

Using the quality control issue as an example, if problems occur at a lower level in the organization—whether during initial intake, data entry, or sourcing components for your product—the leader needs to be aware of them and address them as quickly as possible. Perhaps the components being sourced are not up to spec or are ineffective in some way. You can create a more efficient process for sharing important information by intentionally improving communication and feedback channels.

For example, some organizations flatten their chain of command to improve communication and increase efficiency. In some cases, you may implement a process where specific communications come directly to you instead of passing through multiple layers of management. This means the person experiencing the issue—perhaps someone at a lower level—can report the problem directly to you.

This way, you hear it unfiltered, see the issue firsthand, and can take immediate action to fix it. Strong communication and feedback channels are essential to addressing concerns quickly rather than allowing them to move through a slow chain of command where it might take days or weeks to reach your desk. By the time the issue finally reaches you, the original message may have been altered, or worse, the delay may have allowed the problem to escalate into something more difficult to solve.

Reliable and effective communication and feedback channels not only help leaders identify and address urgent company issues but also provide insight into areas where leadership itself can improve. Some companies use surveys to gather feedback on leadership performance, product improvements, cultural growth, customer experiences, or any other topics they want to understand from employees' perspectives.

Some leaders may read this and think, *I would never do this. I know what's best for my company and employees—I don't need to hear what they think.* But the reality is that feedback benefits everyone. If you're in a band and play a show in front of friends, one of the first questions you ask them is, "How did we do?" You want an honest answer because you're looking for ways to improve before the next show. You want to keep getting better and growing your fan base.

But some leaders are afraid of feedback. I believe that's why they avoid asking for it—no one enjoys hearing that they did something wrong, that they're not good enough, or that they made a mistake. We are wired to appreciate positive feedback and dislike negative feedback.

One of the best ways to give and receive feedback effectively is to start with the positive.

You can start with, "What are three things we did well? What are the best things our leadership has done that you'd like us to continue?" Then follow up with, "What are three things we can improve?" Asking the question this way encourages constructive feedback. No matter how good you are, there is always room for improvement.

Leaders who think they're already the best are missing out on valuable feedback that could help them become better leaders and people. Every leader can improve in some way.

As a leader, you deal with different personalities, people with diverse experiences, and individuals from various backgrounds. Because of this broad range of perspectives, your team can offer insights you may not have considered—ideas that could improve your organization in unexpected ways.

If someone has feedback that can help you improve, embrace it. Own it. Welcome it. That's the attitude you need to have as a leader: "Bring it on. Tell me where we can be better—please."

Once you receive feedback, you can decide how to respond. If there are ideas you like, you can develop a plan and execute them. Prioritize the ideas that will have the most significant positive impact on your organization in the shortest period of time. You can also use feedback to refine your leadership style. Remember, we all have blind spots. Maybe the feedback you receive will help you turn one of your blind spots into a clear path for growth. This makes you a more effective leader and shows your team that you are listening and value their input. That's powerful. Now they're thinking, *Whoa, he or she is actually listening to us. They want us to be better. They're hearing everything we're saying. And we like this leader—they're awesome now.*

Another benefit is that your team gains greater respect for you and, in some cases, becomes even more motivated to work harder. It can build loyalty and chemistry because they know their voices are being heard and valued in the organization. That's a powerful dynamic for both you as a leader and for your team members. It can provide valuable help for leaders struggling with performance and productivity issues in their organization and looking for ways to get unstuck.

One key way to adapt your leadership style to optimize team performance is by ensuring you receive the information you need and can act quickly so that issues don't continue harming your organization. Another critical factor is reducing micromanagement. One of the best ways to improve an organization is to empower employees to make certain decisions independently.

Of course, you still need to provide guidelines for decision-making. One example that comes to mind is customer service. If a customer has an issue with a product and wants to return it, you can empower employees to decide in the moment how to resolve the issue and keep the customer happy. You set the rules for this. The ultimate goal is to satisfy the customer. But, of course, there will be cases where the customer is 100% wrong or is attempting to exploit the company in some way. You also need to have a process in place to identify and address those situations.

In some cases, particularly regarding monetary issues, you may implement a policy where small-dollar disputes are resolved immediately. For instance, if a customer wants to return an item that costs less than $10, some companies adopt a policy that states: *If the value is under $20, just refund the money—no questions asked.* That's a leadership decision, and you can see how it can save both time and money. Instead of having your team spend valuable time on the phone or handling low-value customer complaints, you might conduct a cost-benefit analysis and determine that issuing an immediate refund is the most efficient approach. Each company can determine the number that works best for them in addressing customer needs. You want your customers to be happy and to have a positive experience in every aspect of your company, whether it's the product itself, customer service, warranty, or any other interaction. As a leader, your goal is to ensure that your company consistently puts its best foot forward in all of these areas.

When it comes to getting your music tight—which is really important in the context of a band—the more you *practice, practice, practice*, the better your band will become. Before playing a live show, you always want to make sure your band sounds as tight as possible. That means ensuring the timing is perfect—every transition, every intro, and every solo. Everything is 100% in sync, in key, and in time. It should sound like you've practiced the same song a million times. The goal of getting your music tight—being in tune, playing in sync—is to provide the best possible experience for your fans.

I've been in bands where we weren't as tight, maybe because we were new and playing out for the first few times. So the timing might have been slightly off, or we might not have sounded as cohesive as we should have. That's usually the nature of a new or upcoming band, which is fine. But over time, you want to tighten that up.

The next time that customer—someone in the audience—hears you play, you want them to notice the improvement. You want them to hear that you sound tight, in sync, and better than before. That's really the goal of this chapter from a leadership standpoint—you are tightening up aspects of your organization to continually raise the bar and make it better. Ultimately, this improves the customer experience at every level of your organization.

Having considered ways to adapt your leadership style to optimize team performance, we're now ready to begin thinking about building harmony and aligning individual contributions with organizational goals. This is essential because it ensures that employees are on board with making the organization better.

I've found that creating professional development plans for every team member helps you understand where they are, where they want to be, and how you can align their individual goals with the company's objectives. Essentially, each person assesses their strengths and weaknesses, areas for improvement, and intentional growth strategies to optimize their role to collectively benefit the team.

This requires understanding your employees' aspirations—what they want to do, where they see themselves growing, their interests within the organization, and what they want to explore further. For example, when I was an electrical engineering intern in the aviation industry working in artificial intelligence and robotics, I was interested in other areas of the industry as well. Being around airplanes growing up sparked my curiosity, and I wanted to learn as much as possible about them. The aviation internship provided that opportunity.

I was proactive in sharing my interests with my boss, and as a result, I fulfilled my main job responsibilities while also gaining experience elsewhere. I was very fortunate and grateful that they allowed me to do that. Now, I was only an intern at the time, but had I been a full-time employee, my boss and I could have created a professional development plan that mapped out how I could grow and add value while aligning my career development with the company's goals and objectives.

Professional development plans are also critical for succession planning, as they prepare individuals on your team to become leaders who align with the company's mission, values, and purpose. These plans also help retain and attract new talent, thus strengthening your team.

You want your employees to be the best they can be. You hire people with specific skills and experience to help your organization grow. And, just like with a new band member, you want to make sure they fit in. You give them space to improve and the opportunity to shine. As a leader, you have to know when to step in and when to step back. A structured plan for them to grow, maximize their value to the team, and be held accountable provides clarity and a clear path to success. This benefits not only the individual but the entire organization.

It also shows your employees that you care about their growth and success. And believe me, it's worth the time and effort to implement and maintain these plans to ensure that everyone is aligned with your organization's core values and committed to its success.

Exercise: *What band do you think has the best musicians of all time and why?*

I chose this question because, a lot of times, it's not just about the songs—it's about the people behind them. Some bands were formed by musicians who were already highly regarded in their field. Led Zeppelin comes to mind—they were considered some of the best musicians of their time when they came together as a band.

For this chapter, we also have a team-building exercise.

Have each member of your team pick a song they feel will inspire and motivate the group to reach its goals, along with an explanation of why they chose that song and how it relates to the team's success. This will become your *team playlist.*

As you add new team members, have them pick a song to add to the list. The cool part about this exercise is that it allows everyone to contribute to the team's culture. Each song represents a part of them—something they believe will help the team.

It's a beautiful way to foster engagement and make team members feel that they are contributing something meaningful. It also creates an opportunity for camaraderie and chemistry through music. Team members can share stories about the songs and artists that have impacted their lives, making it a great bonding experience. It's also fascinating to see how the playlist reflects the team's culture.

This exercise helps coworkers and leaders get to know each other on a deeper level—learning why someone picked a particular song, why it resonates with them, and why they believe it's effective for the group.

It might also introduce team members to songs or even genres they've never explored. They may even add some of these songs to their personal playlists. I like this exercise because it brings the team together in a unique and meaningful way.

In the next chapter, we'll explore creating a team environment that fosters creativity and innovation. Build a culture that thrives on communication, collaboration, and idea-sharing to fuel operational efficiency, drive product development, and set your organization up for success.

PART V
PILLAR FIVE: WRITING SONGS

9

FINDING THAT NUMBER-ONE HIT

*E*very band that writes its own music wants a number-one hit.
That's the goal. It's similar to an athlete playing football—
they want to compete in the biggest game of the year, every year. For
artists, it's the same way.

How do you find that number-one hit? How do you write the one song
that completely changes your life? A lot of that comes from creativity. We
talked earlier about *practice, practice, practice*. We talked about finding ideal
people for your team who buy into your mission, values, and purpose.

If you do all of those things, there's a good chance you've assembled a
band where everyone shares the same vision. You all aspire to be great.
You all dream of becoming rock stars one day.

And you all want to write that number-one hit together. You've built
the team, developed chemistry, and put in the practice. Now, it's time to
show what each of you can do collectively to create that hit song.

The way to do that is by fostering an environment that encourages
creativity and innovation. If you talk to different musicians, they'll tell
you about the various methods they use to find inspiration and write
songs. Songwriting can be a collaboration between two or more band
members. There could also be one primary songwriter who writes everything and presents the songs to the rest of the group. Sometimes, one

band member will come up with an idea and bring it to the group, and the band will shape that idea into a full song. Other times, the entire band gets in a room and starts jamming, recording the session as they go. They riff, experiment, and explore ideas together.

This is where chemistry is crucial—when you understand your bandmates, you can anticipate what they'll do next. Someone might play something unexpected, and you think, *Ooh, I can play off that*—maybe by adding a guitar riff, a drum fill, or a bass groove. Maybe the singer hears something that sparks an idea—something personal, something meaningful, or a message the band wants to share with its audience. Love, family, loss, or major life experiences are the inspiration for many songs. Sometimes, the music itself inspires the lyrics. You've probably heard the story about Guns N' Roses—how Slash used to practice the opening riff to "Sweet Child O' Mine" until Axl Rose, after hearing it, wrote the lyrics for the song. That's just one example.

The key is building an environment that stimulates innovation and maximizes your team's creative potential.

If you're in business, think of ways to create space for your team to be creative, to motivate and inspire them to share ideas. Give them opportunities to actively contribute to the company's vision and mission. Get them excited to come to work and gain valuable experience to help them grow in their careers. Empower them to take initiative, take ownership of their roles, and make meaningful contributions to the team. Encourage them to ask, *What if we did this to improve our business, product, or team?* And most importantly, give them space to try—and fail.

Encourage them to experiment and explore new ideas without the fear of failure holding them back. Fear of failure is one of the biggest obstacles to progress, both for organizations and individuals. Inspire your team to take risks and try new things, and provide them with structure and guidance to ensure that they're channeling their creativity effectively.

You want to ensure that your team makes informed decisions, with a high likelihood that what they attempt will actually work. And when they fail, they should learn from those failures. Document those failures. Dissect them. *Why did we fail? How can we do this better next time to avoid failing again?* This approach allows you to foster continuous creativity, innovation, and feedback. By leveraging the collective intelligence of your team, you can improve your products, projects, or any other initiative you're working on together.

You also want to constantly motivate, inspire, and, in some cases, offer incentives for improvement. As a songwriter, you receive publishing rights—if you write a song, you get credit for it. In music, that's important. Some bands give songwriting credit to every member, while others assign credit only to one or a few members. That concept of recognition can serve as an incentive in music. Similarly, in your organization, there may be ways to recognize and reward employees who contribute creative ideas or innovations. Push your team to strive for that incredibly difficult-to-achieve number-one hit. Maybe they receive an award, a monetary bonus, additional paid time off—whatever fits your company's culture. Providing incentives encourages creativity and innovation.

You also want to establish a clear process for collaboration and idea-sharing. This process might include meeting guidelines designed to optimize creativity and ensure that ideas are shared effectively. One of the biggest time wasters in many companies is meetings—especially when people are meeting just for the sake of meeting. There should be clear guidelines on conducting meetings, their length, how participants prepare beforehand to maximize productivity, and whether recurring meetings should continue or not.

Some meetings are set to repeat automatically, and no one stops to ask whether they're still necessary. If a meeting has lost its purpose, you may no longer be fostering collaboration; instead, it becomes an obligation. You show up, go through the motions, and leave feeling like your time was wasted. Meetings can interrupt meaningful work, becoming more of a distraction than a benefit to the team. That's why it's crucial to ensure that every opportunity for collaboration is optimized and truly valuable.

Collaboration should not feel like a chore. It should not feel like an obligation that adds no value, creativity, or inspiration to the work your team is doing. If it does, it could actually hinder creativity instead of fostering it. That's why it's essential to have a structured process for collaboration and sharing innovative ideas.

It all starts with leadership. As a leader, you must provide your team with the tools and resources needed to be creative and innovative. This can include software tools for brainstorming, idea collection, and group evaluation. It's also important to establish clear communication and feedback channels where ideas can flow freely—without fear of judgment or ridicule. One of the biggest reasons people hesitate to share their ideas—whether in meetings or other group settings—is fear. If they voice an idea and someone immediately shuts it down or dismisses it as silly, they become less likely to contribute in the future. The more negative responses they receive, the less they will offer their ideas and opinions. The last thing you want to do as a company—or as a leader—is create an environment that stifles creativity, discourages questions, or makes people afraid to share feedback. Your role is to foster a culture of open communication, welcoming ideas so that every team member feels empowered to speak up.

Silencing your team means cutting off valuable communication and feedback channels that could improve your products and services, increase operational efficiency, give your company a competitive advantage, or enhance the customer experience. You've also cut off creativity, which hurts your organization because the people with great ideas will never voice them. They will never share their thoughts for fear of being ridiculed, demeaned, or made to feel insignificant. So, you definitely want to keep those channels open and encourage your team to use them.

Songwriting provides a great demonstration of this idea in music. When an artist releases an album, we hear the final product—the polished songs they've chosen to share with the world. What we *don't* hear are the hundreds or even thousands of songs they started, experimented with, or set aside. They are constantly creating, writing, and rewriting. Behind the scenes, they are always innovating, coming up with new ideas, and drawing inspiration from the world around them. They find creative sparks in their relationships, the ups and downs of life, what they see on TV or social media, and events happening around them. These experiences fuel their creativity and help them capture those magical moments—what artists often refer to as *lightning in a bottle*.

Every songwriter dreams of creating that *magic moment*—when a sudden burst of inspiration turns into an idea, a melody, or a lyric that builds into a song. And if everything aligns, that song could turn into a hit —or, even better, a number-one hit. That's why it's important to create an environment and structure that fosters creativity and innovation, ensuring your team has the opportunity to capture ideas as they come.

Any songwriter will tell you that song ideas can pop up at any time, in any place. You could be sleeping, riding the subway, sitting in a restaurant, attending a wedding, or alone at home after a breakup. Inspiration can strike anywhere. And in that moment, you think, *This is a number-one hit.* Realistically, it may never be a hit—statistically, you'd have a better chance of winning the lottery—but in *your* head, at *that* moment, you believe in it. And that's why you need to capture it.

It could be lost forever if you don't write it down or otherwise record the idea immediately. You might think, *I'll remember it tomorrow, and that's when I'll record it.* But how many times have you had an idea, only to find that it's gone when you try to recreate it later? I can't tell you how many times I've had an idea in my head, only to forget it when I tried to recall it later. I think about what it *might* have been or what I *thought* it was, but it never feels quite the same. The magic from that moment is lost.

So, if your team has a creative idea or a sudden spark of inspiration, provide them with the resources and tools to capture it *in the moment.* Then, ensure they have a way to communicate those ideas to the team for consideration. This is crucial because creativity isn't something you can force—it has to come naturally. Sometimes, it's triggered by things we see, hear, or experience. That's why it's important to make sure your team members capture their ideas, share them, and use them to help improve the team and the company as a whole.

You also want to empower your team to be curious and think of better ways to do their job or provide better solutions for your customers. You have the structure in place, but how can you actually pull those ideas out of your team? This may include scheduling brainstorming sessions where team members can share their captured ideas or generate new ones. You might also implement a virtual *idea jar* where employees can submit a wide range of ideas—from small improvements in daily tasks to big ideas that could reshape your product or company direction.

The key is to capture as many good ideas as possible. We all innovate daily, even if we don't consciously think about it. We're always looking for ways to be more efficient. We tend to buy products like coffee makers, air fryers, or other time-saving tools based on this behavior. We're constantly looking for ways to shorten our commute, such as finding a back road that saves five minutes. If we need to paint a house, we might choose a spray painter instead of a brush to do the job faster. We buy organizers and download productivity apps to better manage our time and be more productive in daily life.

At work, it's the same way. You're constantly innovating. You're always thinking of ways to improve a product or optimize your job to make routine tasks more efficient. This could involve delegation—passing off certain tasks so that you have more time to focus on creative and strategic work.

As a leader, you should constantly look for ways to inspire and motivate your team to generate ideas that drive innovation. These ideas can improve products, services, or even daily workflows. And who better to generate those ideas than the smart people you hired to handle these tasks every day? The employees who design and make your products interact with customers daily, focus on revenue growth, manage your P&Ls, and protect your company's data and intellectual property.

You need big and small ideas to keep your company innovating and growing. You also need a system to capture and vet those ideas, ensuring you extract the ones that will impact your organization the most.

Gamification can be a great way to motivate and inspire your team to be innovative while making the process fun. For example, using a music analogy, you could categorize submitted ideas over 12 months as a *Top 100 Hit, Top 50 Hit, Top 10 Hit,* or a *Number-One Hit.* An idea that suggests using productivity tools to increase operational efficiency by 2% might be considered a *Top 100 Hit,* while an idea that improves your product offering and results in a 20% increase in profitability could be classified as a *Number-One Hit.*

As the leader, you can decide who determines which ideas are adopted and how they are categorized. It could be you, your leadership team, or a committee of employees from different departments. At the end of each 12-month period, you can review which employees contributed the most ideas implemented by the company based on the number of *hits* in each category. The person with the most *hits* near the top of the charts wins!

You can recognize winners from each department and an overall winner with rewards such as monetary incentives, additional time off, free lunch, or other perks.

Choosing which ideas to adopt doesn't have to be difficult. You'll want to create a quick and efficient vetting process to determine which ideas are worth further evaluation. An individual or a committee can handle this. As the leader, you might select the top three ideas you believe are the best and then have the team vote on those finalists. Whatever process you create to filter ideas should be transparent, quick, and fair. For example, establish three clear criteria each idea must meet to warrant further consideration (transparent), assign a deadline of within ten business days (quick), and ensure that every good idea is considered, regardless of who submitted it (fair). This guarantees that everyone has an opportunity to participate and, more importantly, win. And a win for them is a win for your company!

Some of the greatest songs in the world were born from artists sharing ideas. I mentioned Guns N' Roses as an earlier example. Think about Andy Summers' guitar riff in "Every Breath You Take" by The Police— another instantly recognizable, timeless riff. The second you hear it, you know it. Then there's the bass line from "Another One Bites the Dust" by Queen or Chic's "Good Times"—both iconic contributions to hit songs. And how about the drums in Genesis's "In the Air Tonight"? Epic. When you hear that song, you can *feel* the drums—especially that legendary drum riff in the middle of the song that makes it come alive. You know the one.

You'd love for your idea to be the one that makes your product better, strengthens your organization, or—if you're a musician—makes your song a hit. As a leader, your job is to encourage those creative ideas. Who knows? Maybe you'll find that one riff that takes you over the top and gets you a hit record.

Exercise: *(Answer honestly) Does your current leadership style encourage and empower your team to share creative and innovative ideas that improve your products and increase operational efficiency? If not, what are three steps you can take to maximize and manage the flow of ideas from your team?*

Take this exercise seriously. If you're unsure or can't be honest with yourself, ask your team—directly or through an anonymous survey.

Not every leader likes to ask for help, but great leaders encourage it. They welcome input from their team because it's the only way to improve. Otherwise, you're operating in a vacuum. Remember the saying, *Two heads are better than one?* The more ideas you collect, the more opportunities you create for your organization to grow.

Exercise: *What song do you think has the greatest lyrics of all time, and why?*

There are countless songs with incredible lyrics. I can think of plenty. We all have songs with lyrics that inspire us. Write down the one song you believe has the greatest lyrics based on your experiences and the music you love, and explain why. Why do those lyrics connect with you? How do they speak to you?

You might even find that reflecting on these lyrics sparks something in you as a leader—something that could resonate with your team.

In the next chapter, we'll look into identifying what makes your products special. What is it about your products that resonates most with your customers, and how can you use that information to keep putting out "hits"? Read on to find out.

10

KEEPING YOUR SONGS ON THE CHARTS

One of the most difficult challenges for a band, musician, or artist is keeping their music on the charts—staying relevant and consistently releasing popular albums and songs. It's hard to write number-one hits all the time, but for most artists, the goal is to reach the top ten or top twenty, or at least break into the top 100.

You want to be consistently on the charts because, in many ways, it defines you as a band. Many of the greatest bands of our era have charted multiple times, constantly putting out music that keeps them relevant and keeps fans coming back for more. The goal is repeated success.

You're always learning—studying what makes a hit song a hit. What's the life cycle of a hit song? What makes a hit record a hit record? It starts with what appeals to the audience, not necessarily what the band thinks is their best song.

What is the magic of your music—or other popular music—that keeps fans wanting more? What makes it special? Many factors can make a band or song unique enough to sustain success. Some bands, like Pink Floyd or the Grateful Dead, have a distinctive style or aura that sets them apart. It can be difficult to pinpoint or replicate whatever that *magic* is, which is why there are so many one-hit wonders.

Countless bands have managed to capture lightning in a bottle once but have spent the rest of their careers trying to do it again—chasing another hit record but falling short or never charting again. Why is that? Why can't they continue writing hit songs? You would think that if a band has the chemistry and the ability to write a hit song once, they should be able to do it again. What holds them back from keeping their songs on the charts? Why can't they chart consistently? For some, finding that one hit song comes down to trial and error.

I remember watching U2 get inducted into the Rock & Roll Hall of Fame in 2005. I'll never forget The Edge's speech—he talked about the magic of the moment and how it's impossible to predict when it will happen, but the band is always willing to wait for it. And for U2, those magic moments have resulted in several hit songs over the decades. The Edge's speech resonated with me on many levels. He's right—creating that magic isn't something you can force. You can't just sit down and decide, *Today, we're going to write something magical.* It's like what I mentioned earlier—artists often write hundreds of songs, but only a select few make the album. The audience only hears the *best* songs; they don't hear all the others that never see the light of day. A lot of it is trial and error—a constant search for that *one* special song.

Sometimes, while chasing that magical song, an artist may write something they don't think is a hit—only to discover later that it *is* a hit. It all comes down to recognizing what resonates with the audience. You might create something you think is incredible, or you might dismiss an idea, believing it's not strong enough. But then the audience hears it, and it takes off. There are plenty of examples in music history of this happening. For instance, there's the famous story about Radiohead and their song "Creep"—a song they didn't believe would be a hit, yet it became one of their most iconic tracks.

I've read that Nirvana's "Smells Like Teen Spirit" almost didn't make it onto their album. The same goes for the Rolling Stones' "(I Can't Get No) Satisfaction"—I read somewhere that they believed the song wasn't commercial enough to sell. These are just a few examples of how artists have written songs that, in their minds, weren't hits but ultimately became massive successes.

So, as an organization, how do you capture that magic and repeatedly stay on the charts? And how can you learn from things that have become a hit? Well, I think part of it is listening to your audience—paying attention to critics, reviews, and anything people say about your products. Develop a deep understanding of what it is about your products that resonates most with your customers. Is it the brand? A specific feature? Simplicity and ease of use? The price point? Maybe your product is more affordable than your competitors' so consumers keep choosing it. It's crucial to put in the work to understand what keeps your product relevant in the marketplace and to be open to all types of feedback. Sometimes, you might believe your product is popular for one reason, but your customers love it for an entirely different reason.

That's why you need to keep your ear to the ground, always paying attention to what matters most to your customers and what doesn't. You want to keep producing *hits*—creating products that continue to chart and remain popular with your audience. This comes through trial and error, constant innovation, and a relentless drive to improve.

This all ties back to what we discussed earlier in the book—your foundation. First, you establish core principles, put together the right bandmates based on those principles, develop strong chemistry, practice and collaborate to improve, and work so well together that you feed off each other's energy and creativity. Then, as you grow, you put yourself in the best position to keep innovating and creating those magical moments that result in hits.

You want to gather as much data as possible to increase the probability that your product will continue to be a hit—that it will keep resonating with customers and attracting new fans. That's how you ensure you're innovating to meet customer needs, staying creative, and continuously delivering what your audience wants.

Another key factor is staying focused on optimizing and improving your products. We talked about magic—that one thing that truly resonates with customers. You need to make sure you keep giving them more of that —because that's what they want. It's the same with a band. If your fans love guitar solos and you have an incredible lead guitarist, keep giving them guitar solos. If your singer's high notes get the crowd roaring, keep delivering those high notes. If you have a phenomenal drummer like Neil

Peart from Rush, keep giving fans those amazing drum solos. Keep giving them what they love, and they'll keep coming back for more—bringing their friends with them.

Understanding the magic and using it to make your products better and more popular is just the first step. How will you use that magic to truly transform and improve your product?

You know what customers love—a particular feature or a unique selling point—but how can you continue to innovate and use that to evolve your product offerings? Maybe you can develop new products or create service offerings around your existing ones. Maybe there are additional ways to optimize what you're doing—leveraging that one standout feature that truly resonates with your customers to grow your brand and expand your business.

As I mentioned before, as a guitar player growing up in the '80s, I was a big fan of Eddie Van Halen. He set the bar for rock guitarists during that era. If you could play like him, you were in demand. The thing about Eddie that stood out the most to me was his constant innovation. When Van Halen released new songs, I couldn't wait to hear what Eddie's next guitar solos would sound like. It wasn't just about playing fast notes—there was creativity and thought behind it. There was melody. One of the greatest musical pieces I've ever heard is "Eruption. When I first heard "Eruption," it blew me away. I think that was probably the case for many people, musicians or not.

To this day, I still consider it one of the greatest musical pieces ever created. It was revolutionary—nobody had ever done anything like that before. It showcased his innovative tapping techniques and completely changed how people thought about the electric guitar. It was unbelievable. But what made Eddie truly special was that he never stopped innovating. His constant evolution as a guitarist was evident when he wrote the solo for Michael Jackson's "Beat It." In my opinion, that ended up being one of his best guitar solos ever.

As a company, you want to constantly innovate to find your "Eruption" moment—your magic. What can you do differently that you're not doing now? How can you be truly disruptive in your industry? How can you create an even bigger impact with your product in the marketplace or with the services you provide to customers?

It's easy to become complacent and rest on your laurels once you've achieved some success. But the real question is: *How do you sustain success? How do you keep your customers engaged and wanting more?* One way is to consistently innovate, as we discussed in Chapter 9. Give your team the space and environment to be creative. Create communication and feedback channels that allow innovative ideas to flow. You also want to listen to your customers. Gather as much feedback and input as possible to understand what makes your product magical—what resonates with them, what makes them feel a connection to your brand, and what keeps them coming back for more.

By using a strong feedback loop, you avoid the mistake of simply trying to *stay on the charts* for the sake of staying on the charts. You're not just chasing trends or following what's currently popular. Instead, you're truly tuned in—deeply understanding what your customers want while staying aligned with your company's mission, values, and purpose. Some companies just follow trends. But you want to be the *trailblazer*. You want to *set* the trends—not be the *me-too* company that simply follows them.

And if you truly have an innovative product that sets you apart, you must keep raising the bar and leading your space. Success comes down to not only finding the hits but also having more hit records than your competitors. If you consistently produce more hits than them, you will be more successful than them.

To ensure you have more hits than your competitors, you must always keep an eye on what they're doing. Even if you have a number-one hit this year and are at the top of the charts, your competitor might have a number-one hit next year, putting them ahead of you in the market. So, what are you doing to stay ahead and remain there? This is where knowing your magic—what makes you special—comes into play. What is the one feature, or combination of features, that makes your products and services superior to the competition? Creativity and innovation can help you improve those features and maintain a competitive advantage.

Understanding your competitors' products is also critical, as it allows you to explain clearly to customers why your products are the better choice for their needs. You don't just want to stay ahead of the competition—you want to increase your market share. Capturing as much market share as possible benefits not only your team and company in terms of revenue but also your shareholders and other stakeholders. That's why you should always focus on three key things:

1. What makes your products special (how do they address your customers' needs)?
2. What is your competition doing?
3. How can you leverage your product's strengths to expand your market share?

This knowledge allows you to create other products incorporating that magic or offer services built around it, generating additional revenue streams and deeper connections with your customers. How can you constantly innovate and push boundaries? How can you continue to amaze customers with what you offer today while also creating new *magic* for the future?

In some ways, every song that hits the charts has its own magic—even from the same band or artist. It may resonate with fans in a fresh, unexpected way. The same applies to your business—every new product or service you introduce has the potential to captivate your customers in a way that builds excitement and loyalty.

Exercise:
1. What is the biggest step you are taking (or should take) to ensure that you are meeting or exceeding your customers' needs?
2. What is the biggest step you are taking (or should take) to stay ahead of the competition?
3. What is the biggest step you are taking (or should take) to increase your market share?

For question #1: This question is important because it requires you to reflect deeply on how you can progress toward your goal of delivering what your customers want and keeping your products on the charts.

For question #2: To answer this question, you need to have a firm understanding of what your competitors are doing, and what you need to do to maintain a competitive edge in your industry. Think about what step you can take now that will have the most impact on building your lead.

For question #3: There are several steps you can take to increase market share - innovating new technologies, selling through new channels, increasing customer loyalty, and acquiring other companies, just to name a few. Determine which path works best for your company to boost market share in your industry.

> **Exercise:** *If you could only listen to one song for the rest of your life, what would it be and why?*

I chose this question because it's similar to the classic desert island scenario—if you were stranded and could only take one song with you, which would you choose?

Try to identify the magic in that song. What is it that keeps you wanting to listen to it over and over again? If you can pinpoint that magic, you may be able to apply similar principles to your company and business. Understanding what makes something irresistible to people can help you recognize the *magic* in what you do—and, more importantly, how to replicate it as your organization grows.

In the next chapter, we'll explore how to build confidence and consistency as a leader and actively listen to your team to hear when things are out of tune. Having stage presence is critical to being a better leader, not only to motivate and inspire your team, but to give your customers and stakeholders the best experience you have to offer.

PART VI
PILLAR SIX: PERFORMING LIVE

11

SHOWING STAGE PRESENCE

This chapter is very important when it comes to leadership. You want to show *stage presence*. You want to be seen as a leader. You want to take control and build confidence and trust within your team and among your customers.

One of the most inspiring things about musicians is their ability to perform night after night on long, grueling world tours. Every evening, they step onto a stage in a different city, in front of thousands of new people, and they *have* to bring it—*every night*. You can't call in sick. You can't say, "I don't feel like performing tonight." As the saying goes in show business, "The show must go on."

As a leader, you have to be the one who continues to inspire and motivate your team to perform at their best, even in difficult moments. That's the true test of leadership. If the leader doesn't want to be there, doesn't put on a good show, or lacks enthusiasm and energy, it's tough for the team to deliver their best performance. And the worst part? *The audience notices.*

When artists perform live, the audience gives instant feedback. If they're not feeling the performance, they'll let you know. They'll boo. Sometimes, they'll throw things on stage. And they're not shy about it—they'll make it clear: *You're not bringing it tonight, and we don't like it.*

The ultimate message an audience sends when they're disappointed? They walk out. They don't care if the band is exhausted. They don't care if the musicians aren't in the mood that night. They spent their hard-earned money; they expect to be entertained.

If you're the leader of the band, you're the first person they'll blame. As a leader, you not only have to deliver for the audience, but you also have to make sure your *band* is ready to perform at its best—even if they are exhausted or haven't had a good night's sleep in two months. That's *not* the audience's problem. It's *yours*—as the leader.

So when your bandmates say things like, "I don't know if I have the energy to perform tonight" or "My fingers are still bleeding from the last show," it's your job to find a way to motivate them. I've played with drummers whose fingers would bleed from gripping their drumsticks too tightly. They'd wrap them in Band-Aids just to keep going. You could see the pain on their faces, but they still had to perform. That's where great leadership comes in—knowing what to do and say in the moment to help your teammate push through.

The show must go on—that goes for business, too. Whether it's your relationship with your team, customers, investors, board, or other stakeholders, you need to perform for them every day, no matter what else is going on. Every day, you need to bring the energy and confidence your audience expects. You need to know how to effectively handle anxiety and pressure every time you take the stage.

That stage could be:

- A meeting with your team
- A presentation to investors or shareholders
- A Zoom call with your board
- A pitch to a major client
- A conversation with a top executive you're trying to recruit
- A keynote speech at a conference
- A product showcase for influencers and the media

No matter the situation, you have to act like a leader. The spotlight can never be too bright for you—from the first song to the encore. And then, you have to be ready to do it all again the next day. You always have to be ready for what comes next.

So how can you perform at a high level every time? A good start is to lean on the core principles you established for your team—mission, values, and purpose. Know your mission, live your values, and never forget your purpose—your why. These principles will carry you through both good times and bad.

Also, apply the lessons from the chapter on *practice, practice, practice.* The more you practice, the more prepared you'll be. Being a leader who is in control isn't difficult if you're ready for the moment. Even in times of uncertainty, preparation helps you make sound decisions under pressure. Whether you're a guitarist, a professional athlete, or the CEO of a Fortune 50 company, *practice, practice, and more practice* will make you better and prepare you for your biggest challenges.

It helps you grow, strengthens your bond with your team, and builds the confidence you need to lead when it matters most. And everyone is watching when the spotlights are trained on you. In those moments, your audience will decide whether you are a strong leader—the leader they believe can take the company where it needs to go. That's why stage presence and performing live as a leader are so important. You need to show that you can lead effectively, give your customers what they want, inspire and motivate your team to perform at their best, and build trust with all the people who rely on you—even when times are tough and things aren't going well.

Some musicians still get nervous before taking the stage—even after performing for years. It's fascinating to read or watch interviews where artists admit, "Oh yeah, I still get nervous," even after playing a thousand shows. Walking onto that stage in front of thousands of fans still brings the butterflies. Part of that is what we discussed earlier—the fear of failure. No artist wants to walk onstage and embarrass themselves in front of their fans. And now, with audiences recording every live show on their phones, everything an artist does—good or bad—will end up on social media for the world to see. The anxiety is real. We're all wired to feel anxious in high-stakes moments. Again, fear of failure is one of the biggest triggers of that anxiety. Seasoned artists rely on their talent and experience to pull them through, night after night, no matter the situation. Even with anxiety, they still go out there and perform at the highest level, inspiring their bandmates to do the same.

In 2023, I remember watching a video of Blink-182 performing at Coachella. I was impressed by their show and their new music, but even more impressed by the genuine support they showed for each other. Each band member had been through a lot over the years, which is well-documented, but the energy they brought to that performance—outdoors, in the desert—was remarkable. Talk about a band with incredible stage presence. You could see how dialed in they were that night—how tight they were as a band. They ensured that everyone who bought a ticket to Coachella that day got their money's worth. Those are the kinds of bands that overcome adversity and bring it. Those are the kinds of artists leaders can learn from.

You want to be a consistent leader whether times are good or bad—and you will experience both. There will be stretches where things are *really* bad—where you face one challenge after another and deal with wave after wave of bad news.

And when morale is low, your team will feel it. People might even consider leaving. The grumblings will start. Negativity will spread, and the chemistry you've spent years building will be tested. That's when you must be consistent—relying on the core values and principles that define your leadership. You must be unwavering in your message, reassuring your team that, even though times are tough, "We will pull through together as a team."

As a leader, when the spotlight is on you, that's when you need to shine. Always remember to be consistent. Show strength in times of uncertainty and chaos. It's okay to show empathy. It's okay to show that you're human. Being human and relatable will help you connect with your team when they need it most. But when the lights go on, make sure you're ready to lead, inspire, and perform at a high level. Your audience expects it.

What helps leaders maintain consistency in their messaging is what we have emphasized throughout this book—alignment with your mission, values, and purpose. This applies not only to the leader but to everyone in the company. When I think of my favorite artists and bands, I admire them because of the music they create. I know that when they release a new album, it will be good because they are consistent. I know what to expect from them. Whatever first connected me to their music remains intact with each new song or album they release. And when they perform live, they consistently put on an amazing show. They bring energy and excitement and always leave their fans wanting more.

I'll never forget the first time I watched *U2 Live at Red Rocks: Under a Blood Red Sky.* I was a student at the University of Virginia, and one of the guys in the dorm invited a group of us to his room to watch the film. Before U2 performed "Sunday Bloody Sunday," our freshman host, in his best Bono voice, mimicked Bono's opening line to the song—and then the drums started. Larry Mullen Jr., U2's drummer, began pounding away in a military-style rhythm, setting the tone for what was about to unfold. Then, The Edge played that iconic riff.

As Bono began singing, the song came alive. When Adam Clayton's bass entered the mix, it took the song to an even higher emotional level. Bono's stage presence stood out to me the most that first time—and every time I've watched it since. His command of the stage. His command of the band. His command of the audience. With every lyric, every movement, you could feel Bono's energy. You could feel the band's passion for the song's message. And when Bono brought out a flag and got the audience chanting "No more! No more!" with him, it became something greater than a performance—it became a movement.

Every U2 show I've seen since then carries that same passion and energy. They have been consistent—in their music, message, and presence. Their songs continue to inspire. They bring people together. They give people hope. As a fan, you know what to expect from U2, yet they still leave you wanting more. Their magic has stood the test of time. It resonates across generations, cultures, and backgrounds. Not everyone can be Bono, but you can learn from him and other artists with enormous stage presence. Find something in their leadership that you can apply to yours.

Part of being a leader is listening to your team. You want to get in the habit of practicing active listening to ensure that everybody on your team stays in tune.

It goes back to communication and feedback, as discussed previously. I've dealt with a lot of leaders. I've seen leaders who don't communicate well with their team—they might be busy, frustrated, or thinking about a million other things. I've seen what happens when leaders don't listen to their team the way they should. You can see the frustration from the team members. They want to perform at their best and may have questions, need information, or want to provide input on an important matter, but they get shut down by their boss or others in the organization. It's so important for leaders to be available to their team members when needed. It's also important for leaders to ask questions and listen to what their team is saying back to them.

Practice active listening. Give your team members your full attention when they are speaking to you, and ask clarifying questions to ensure complete understanding. Don't be dismissive or defensive. That's a sure-fire way to cut off valuable input and feedback from your people. The more you shut them down when they offer an idea, an opinion, feedback, or ask a question, guess what? The less they will give feedback, ask questions, or provide opinions. And now you're cutting off some of the most valuable information you can receive from your team. Not only does it make your team less productive, but it also hurts the chemistry and trust you've worked so hard to build as a leader. So, listen to what they're saying. Be responsive. Show emotional intelligence and empathy. You don't have to do everything they ask you to do. You can take what they ask and think about the response you need to give them to motivate and inspire them to be the best they can be.

But sometimes, you have to say no, and there's nothing wrong with that. It's part of being an authentic leader. But you do that in a way that says to them: "Thank you for offering the feedback, providing that information, or asking that question. It is very valuable to me. But I think we should go in a different direction, and here's why." Give them the courtesy of that response to show them that you're listening and that they are a valuable part of the team. Most importantly, allow them to continue to give you feedback. You never know when they will give you an idea or ask a question that sparks something in you—something that makes you realize, "Wow, that was a great idea that's going to make us better as a team and as an organization."

Very important. Also, when you are listening, listen for signs of doubt. Listen for a lack of confidence. Listen for signs of trust issues. Listen for disruptive behavior or signs that someone on your team is struggling. Something may be going on in one of your team members' personal lives that's affecting their work. Listen for that. When you hear something that sounds out of tune or not in sync with the rest of the team, take the time to address it—and address it quickly. Don't wait.

Do not let it get to the point where it's irreparable, where that person may want to leave or potentially spoil the well by talking to others. If they're disgruntled and sharing their feelings with others, those others may start to see things from their point of view. Now, you have a disruption in the team that will undermine the team's chemistry. So, make sure you address it swiftly, but also be thoughtful in how you address it and communicate back to your team.

You also want to train your employees and other members of your leadership team to be active listeners. You want to make sure that they are listening to what the rest of the team is saying. Your communication and feedback channels should be structured to ensure that any issues reach your desk quickly so you can address them in a timely and decisive manner.

But you never want to cut off the line of communication because, again, when you do that, you won't know what's going on in your culture, and it can reach a point where it's beyond repair. Every person on your team has a voice and should feel very comfortable sharing it.

Exercise: *List three actions you can take to be a better listener to your team.*

We can all be better listeners. No matter how good a listener you think you are, you should focus on becoming even better. Ask insightful questions or coach your team members in the moment to help them answer the question themselves.

This is where coaching becomes very important. People will come to you with questions, and you can either give them an answer or help them come up with the answer themselves. Once they reach a point where they can start figuring out the answers on their own without always having to ask you, they'll ask fewer questions and make better decisions. Coaching can help improve their thought process—teaching them how to assess a situation and devise a solution. You want a team that is focused on solutions, no matter what the issue or challenge might be. This puts less burden on the leader and empowers your team members to be better.

And it all ties into a succession plan. Ultimately, you want your team members to become leaders. You hire people who may start in lower-level roles in your organization, but the goal is to develop good people and help them grow within the organization. It's important to encourage them to solve their own problems or address the issues and questions they bring up because, as leaders, they'll need to do that. It's a way of training them to start thinking in that direction so they can be more effective when they step into leadership roles.

> **Exercise:** *What is the greatest live music show you have ever seen and why?*

When I meet new people, I sometimes ask them this question, and they immediately go into storytelling—one of the most powerful communication methods. They start telling the story, smiling as they recall how the show impacted them—everything from the stadium to the band, the audience, the songs, the light show, or whatever else stood out. It really brings them out of their shell and breaks the ice.

It gets them to open up about who they are and why they like certain things. This is valuable information for a leader because it helps you understand what motivates and inspires your team. So, you can answer this question yourself, and you can also present it to your team. It's great for team building.

In the next chapter, we'll focus on building a fan base by understanding what your audience wants through information gathering and feedback. This data not only helps companies improve their products, but also provides insights on how to better engage with your customers to build loyalty.

1 2

BUILDING A FAN BASE

*O*ne of the most important goals of a band is to build its fan base. You want to appeal to a broad audience who will buy your music, attend your live shows, and buy your merchandise ("merch," in the industry lingo). You want to go from playing in front of five friends in a garage to playing in front of 30,000 strangers in a stadium—all screaming your name.

That's the goal of any band that wants to make it in music, similar to a company that releases a product or offers a service. You want to start with a small group of fans or customers, but you also want that customer base to grow. So how do you do that? How do you build a fan base? How do you get people excited about your product and what you're doing? How do you get people excited about your music and your songs? When you're relatively unknown, it's very difficult. For artists starting out, it means taking any gig you can get—paid or not—and selling merch out of your trunk.

In one of my college bands, we got paid with beer, not money, but it didn't matter because we just wanted to perform and get in front of as many people as possible. The more we played live, the more fans we picked up, and the better we got as a band. It was awesome having people you didn't know come up to you after a show and give you positive feedback. It made you want to keep improving and playing more shows.

Nowadays, one way to quickly build a fan base is to go viral on social media. Platforms like TikTok and Instagram allow artists and other content creators to become instantly popular overnight—for better or for worse. Just like artists write songs hoping they'll be a number-one hit, influencers post on TikTok, hoping their content goes viral and is seen by millions of people worldwide. It's all trial and error, though. You don't know what songs will become number-one hits or what TikTok video will go viral, but you keep trying, hoping to capture that magic moment for the world to see.

I think many brands struggle with who they are and what they think will resonate with their fans, so they just throw stuff at the wall—"Oh, let's try this and see if it works." Or they see what someone else posts on TikTok that goes viral and say, "Let's just copy them, and maybe we'll go viral too." But capturing that magic in the moment is hard to do. You can't force somebody to be creative on demand and expect success. Creativity happens organically for many—that brilliant idea comes to you while you're showering, dreaming at night, or hiking a mountain trail. You also can't just copy someone else and expect success. That's not being authentic or in alignment with your mission, values, and purpose.

The beauty of fans is that they immediately know when you're not being authentic—and they're not afraid to let you know about it. It's like being around children with no filter, telling it like it is. If you've been working out at the gym and need a shower, your kids will tell you, "Dad, you stink!" My point is that your fans will keep you honest. They will let you know if they like your product, your brand, or other things you do. But they will also let you know if you're not being authentic. They will see through it, and it can hurt your brand. There is a balance, and you have to be careful about what you do or how you represent your brand to try to capture a bigger audience—because it could backfire on you.

On a positive note, it's amazing to see artists go viral, whether or not they're famous. I love watching videos on YouTube where you'll see these random artists playing a piano in a mall or a guitar on a street corner.

They start playing a popular song like "Bohemian Rhapsody" by Queen, and suddenly, a crowd forms around them, in awe of how talented they are. It's great to see that because—what's attracting those fans? Is it the choice of song or the skill of the musician? Or maybe a combination of both?

I would argue that the song immediately grabs their attention, while their impression of the artist builds over time. What makes that song resonate so much that you want to stop and listen? Understanding what your audience connects with in your music is crucial. The simple question is: What makes them a fan?

In business, you want to understand why your customers like your products. You can learn this through research, customer reviews, in-person meetings, surveys, conferences, industry events, and more. You want to stay in contact with them through social media, newsletters, and other communication platforms. You need to know where they are, how they consume your product, and how to use that information to find new customers and build your fan base.

Be strategic in how you engage with them. Optimize the fan experience and try to capture them in the moment as they interact with your products. Think about a live concert—when is the best time to sell a concert t-shirt? Right after the concert. If you enjoyed the show, you're still buzzing from the experience and are willing to drop $30 on a t-shirt because you want to keep that high going. You're talking with friends and other fans as you exit the arena, reminiscing about your favorite moments from the show. That's when people make impulsive decisions to extend the excitement as long as possible.

As an artist, you want to keep that fandom experience going for as long and as often as possible. To me, fandom exists at a brand level rather than just a product level. For example, Taylor Swift fans don't just like her music—they love everything about her. They admire how she dresses, how she interacts with her fans, and even her merch. Growing up in the '80s, when Madonna reached stardom, you saw high school girls dressing like her. They learned to dance like her and, in some cases, even talk like her. You saw something similar with Britney Spears in the late 1990s and early 2000s. Building this level of fandom takes years of success, but many artists aspire to reach it.

You also see this in more niche areas of music, where fandom represents a culture. People who love punk rock embrace a lifestyle reflected in their hairstyles and clothing. Some punk rock fans take on the identity of their favorite artists and proudly express it.

In business, you also want to create that level of fandom—where people buy your products, engage with others who love your products, and rep your brand at every opportunity. They want to be associated with your brand and the image it represents. Brands like Patagonia and Apple have achieved this kind of affiliation among their customers.

You want your customers to be all in on everything you do. Your company's values should reflect the values of your customers. In a way, your customers become an extension of your culture and purpose—and they keep wanting more. That's the power of fandom.

One way to build a fandom is to capture people in the moment when they're engaging with your products and enjoying them. For example, if you're a guitar player and you're playing a killer solo live on stage, and you see the audience getting into it, you will want to keep playing the solo to extend the moment you've created for your fans.

A great example of this comes from one of the most iconic performances in the Rock & Roll Hall of Fame induction ceremony history— Prince's legendary guitar solo during "While My Guitar Gently Weeps," a song written by George Harrison and performed by the Beatles. The year was 2004, and it was one of the most amazing performances I'd ever seen during a Rock & Roll Hall of Fame induction ceremony—and I've been watching them for years. On stage with Prince was an all-star lineup, including Tom Petty, Jeff Lynne, and Steve Winwood, and it was an unforgettable moment for many reasons.

First, Prince was being inducted into the Rock & Roll Hall of Fame that year, along with George Harrison (posthumously). That set the stage for this moment to happen, and I'm sure when they came up with the idea to put all of these great artists on stage together, no one knew just how historic that moment would be. Second, Prince was primarily known for his R&B, funk, and dance music, although he had released songs that could be classified as rock. Seeing him perform a guitar solo for a song outside his typical style and playing it so masterfully probably surprised some people. It was also rare to see him collaborate with other well-known artists on stage, especially ones of a different genre.

But he was asked to perform that night, and I'm sure he shocked some people with just how great of a guitar player he was. Near the end of the song, Prince began his solo, immediately captivating the audience. The beauty of that moment was that while Prince played, he also connected with his fellow musicians on stage. Tom Petty looked at him and motioned for him to keep going. They all seemed to recognize in real-time that they were sharing something special—one of the most memorable performances in Rock & Roll Hall of Fame history. Prince kept playing until the song ended, and that moment became just that—one of the most iconic in the show's history.

Why is that so important? It ties into building your fan base by capturing those magical moments and knowing when to extend them. Recognizing when your audience is fully engaged allows you to create something special that you can even replicate later. If you perform a killer guitar solo on stage for one audience and it goes over well, maybe you do it in subsequent shows so that other fans can experience that moment for themselves. The same applies to business—you want to find those elements that keep your customers engaged and excited about interacting with your product.

Get to know and understand your customers' feelings when they're using your product in the moment. This helps you further engage them and build your fan base by gathering valuable insights. In a musical context, I've seen artists use techniques to keep fans engaged, like holding the mic out to the audience and having them sing a section of the song or the chorus. That interaction excites the audience and deepens their connection to the performance. The business equivalent would be identifying what customers love about your product and amplifying that experience. If customers rave about a certain feature, maybe you highlight one of them in a promotional video where they can tell their story and share a genuine moment about how your product made a difference in their life. Those stories might resonate with other fans who have had similar experiences with your product, helping to strengthen their connection to your brand.

Some companies already incorporate this into their marketing by getting fans involved or at least trying to recreate moments of fans experiencing their products in certain situations. This helps engage other fans as well. It's similar to what happens during sporting events when you see beer or chips commercials—products that fans might already be consuming while watching the game. These commercials resonate with fans in the moment, reinforcing their connection to the brand. When a company successfully aligns its messaging with a fan's experience, the attachment to the product deepens. The goal is to capture these moments to keep fans engaged and build a new fan base using those shared experiences and the feedback you receive from customers.

One of the most important types of feedback is negative feedback. Of course, we all want positive feedback—when you put out a product, you want people to say it's great. But for a lot of leaders, checking customer reviews can be a nerve-racking experience, especially when you come across a one-star review. It's easy to overreact to negative feedback, but the reality is that you learn more from it than from positive reviews. Now, you can disregard some negative feedback—there will always be reviews that provide no constructive criticism, and in some cases, reviews might even be fake. However, the reviews that offer well-thought-out criticism are invaluable because they provide insights into why a customer didn't like your product.

Some feedback might reveal that your product is not easy to use or lacks reliability. This ties back to the idea of being better than your competitors. Of course, every company wants to be better than its competition—that's an obvious goal. But the real question is: What are you doing to achieve that? This is where customer feedback becomes crucial. It helps you improve your products, engage your audience more effectively, and gain a competitive edge in the market.

Another reason to pay close attention to negative feedback is that it can provide insight into your competitors' weaknesses. If a competitor has a feature that customers are consistently dissatisfied with, you should be aware of that and use it as an opportunity. You position yourself as a better alternative to customers by addressing not only the criticisms of your own product but also those of your competitors' products. This shows customers that you are listening to their needs and allows you to market directly to your competitor's fan base by offering products that resolve their pain points.

You should have a structured process for identifying and analyzing negative feedback to improve your product. If you receive a negative review, work with your team to understand what the customer didn't like and why, and then determine how you can use that information to improve the product. How can you refine your product or service in a way that turns a negative review into a positive one?

I've seen this happen: a customer initially leaves a negative review. Then, after engaging with the company and experiencing improved service, they update their one-star rating to five stars (or something in between). The goal is to win over your customers. You can't be perfect for everyone, and not everyone falls within your target demographic, but for those who do—your core audience—you need to listen to them. Whether the feedback is good or bad, responding and showing them you are committed to improving their experience builds trust and loyalty.

The same principle applies to music. If you're a band putting out album after album, you want your fans to be excited, so you focus on creating music that fans want to buy and listen to. I remember back when stores like Tower Records were still around—there were lines of people waiting outside for album releases, even in freezing cold temperatures. When you have a loyal fan base, it's incredible what they will do to get their hands on your new product.

How can you develop that level of customer loyalty with what you're trying to sell? How do you get to the point where your customers would literally risk getting frostbite to experience your product? Engaging with your product should be an experience that connects them to your brand, mission, values, and purpose—an experience that creates moments they can share with their friends.

Give them as many of those moments as possible to share, such as dropping a new video on YouTube and letting your fans spread the word: "Hey, they just posted the video for Jelly Roll's new song on YouTube. Here's the link." When fans share their experiences with others, it helps grow your fan base and strengthens their connection to your brand. Eventually, they won't just be loyal fans of your products; they'll be loyal fans of your brand and everything you're trying to build as an organization.

Building a fan base is about more than selling products—it's also about what you do in the community. It ties back to your purpose. Suppose your purpose is to make the world better in some way. In that case, you can live that purpose by being involved in your community, donating your time and money to causes that align with your mission and values, and sponsoring events that bring your team, your fans, and other communities together. Not only do these efforts further your purpose, but they also attract people who want to learn more about your company, products, and services. They bring in new fans who admire your commitment to making a difference.

There are other ways to build your fan base as well. Look for opportunities where your products can be paired with or offered alongside complementary products. For example, customers who purchase audio equipment receive a free 30-day subscription to the software your company developed specifically for that device. You've now introduced your software to a new fan base—people who were already fans of the audio equipment they just bought. If your software is truly a game-changer, those new fans will want to explore other products your company offers. Take the time to seek out brand partnerships or other opportunities to expand the reach of your products and your brand.

> **Exercise:** *List three features of your product that resonate most with customers.*

This exercise helps you truly understand the magic of your product.

Do you really know what resonates with them? Sometimes, it's not what you think, so feedback is important. You might assume customers love the latest shiny new features, but if you read reviews and feedback, you might be surprised to learn that something else stands out to them.

It's similar to our discussion about hit songs. Sometimes, an artist writes a song thinking it's a guaranteed hit, and it flops. Other times, they write a song they don't expect much from, and it reaches number one on the Billboard charts.

So, it's crucial to understand those key features, and the way to do that is by conducting research, engaging with your customers, gathering data, and using it to make improvements that will attract more customers. Spend time with your team analyzing this data and brainstorming creative ways to use it to improve your product.

Again, we talked about creating space for creativity and innovation—always asking:

- What can we do better?
- How can we make our product better?
- What can we do to improve customer experience so we can continue building our fan base?

Follow the feedback from customers, listen to what they want, and then give it to them. If you do that, this exercise will be easy to complete every time.

Exercise: *What was your greatest fan experience and why?*

This could be meeting your idol—maybe you were at an airport and met Post Malone while waiting for a flight. Or maybe you were at a concert and got the chance to go backstage. Or it could simply be an experience you shared with friends at Coachella—where it was a beautiful day, and you were all just vibing in the moment, watching your favorite artist. Describe your greatest fan experience and why it meant so much to you.

In the next chapter, we'll explore how to create products customers can't wait to buy and how leaders can optimize customer experience through product offerings and support. Prioritizing the customer should be top of mind for any leader looking to successfully grow their business.

PART VII
PILLAR SEVEN: RELEASING YOUR MUSIC TO THE WORLD

13

THE ALBUM

*A*lbums don't have the significance they once did. Back in the day, it was all about the album. Of course, people loved going to live shows, but the album was everything when it came to new music. Fans couldn't wait to get their hands on the latest release from their favorite band. As discussed in the last chapter, people would stand in line in the dead of winter just to buy an album as soon as it came out. The goal of any artist was to sell as many albums as possible.

You wanted each album to resonate with your audience—to the point where they were willing to spend their hard-earned money to buy it. For some people, a new album release from their favorite artist was an event. They couldn't wait to purchase it, rush home, and listen to it uninterrupted from beginning to end. They would invite friends over for listening parties, experiencing the new music together. When an album dropped, one or more hits were already playing on the radio, creating excitement and anticipation.

The album gave artists a powerful way to communicate with their fans. The artist poured their soul into the record or CD, and the fans soaked it in through their speakers. That experience reinforced the emotional connection between the artist and their audience. The artist carefully crafted every song on the album as part of their music journey.

In some cases, bands even released double albums because they had more songs than could fit on a single record. But everything about those albums was designed to communicate with fans—to make them feel something at every step of the journey. That was their product.

For companies, every new version of your product or every additional product you release is like a new album. You want to create a buzz around your product, just like artists do with their albums. Get customers to anticipate your product launch or the next big release. Think about how excited you've been waiting for a new album from your favorite band—you want to create that same feeling in your customers through your messaging, product offerings, and brand experience. And then, just like artists, you have to deliver—exceeding expectations and keeping your audience wanting more.

Sometimes, artists release an EP—a shorter collection of three or four songs—or a single before dropping the full album. These are ways to get fans excited and engaged.

So, how can you create or position your product to generate the same kind of buzz? Maybe you offer a teaser version of your product and then give customers the opportunity to buy the full version. Many companies do this by offering trial versions, giving customers a taste of the experience before asking them to commit to the full product. If they want more functionality, a bigger size, or additional features, they have to pay for it.

Whether it's a trial or a full-featured product, you want every customer interaction to feel special. You want them to come back for more. So, how do you keep your customers coming back? Are you thinking more deeply about what you can do to get them excited about your current and upcoming products? How can you exceed their expectations?

One way to ensure customer satisfaction is by ensuring your products have undergone proper testing and are commercially ready. This guarantees that your products are reliable and perform as intended without issues or bugs. It ensures that your customers' needs are met and that all the features they expect are included. This may seem obvious, but I have purchased many products that have failed to meet this basic standard. I can't count how many times I've been disappointed by a product, even after extensive research. It sounds simple, yet some companies still fall short in this area.

If your product meets customers' needs, it strengthens your brand reputation and increases customer engagement. It reassures customers that you're listening to their feedback, anticipating what they want, and delivering it to them. And if you can consistently meet or exceed expectations with your product offerings, you'll stay ahead of the curve and keep your audience engaged—wanting to buy more.

You must also prioritize customer experience in every aspect of your product offering and support. Returning to the album analogy, we couldn't wait to listen to a new album, but it wasn't just about the music. It was about the entire experience: buying the album, ripping off the plastic wrap, admiring the cover art, and smelling the vinyl. It was a ritual. Some album covers had two flaps that opened up. Some included liner notes.

Every part of the experience was intentional. Everything—from the wrapping to the artwork—was carefully designed to give customers the experience they had been waiting for, the one they had stood in line for. It all mattered.

And while you listened to the music, you could immerse yourself in all those elements. I remember experiencing Pink Floyd's *The Wall* album for the first time in college—the album cover, the music, the entire experience. It was unlike anything I had ever listened to before. But it was clear that every detail was intentional—from the artwork to the controversial lyrics to the mind-bending music. That album included one of my favorite songs and guitar solos of all time: "Comfortably Numb." As a guitar player, I connected with the guitar solos immediately. The imagery of the wall from the album cover in my head and the lyrics still resonating in my ears took me to a different level. The experience of that album not only gave the audience what they wanted but also left them wanting more.

That album engaged you from beginning to end; every time you played it, you discovered something new. So, when releasing a product, make sure your product offering prioritizes the entire customer experience with the same level of detail from beginning to end.

It's not just about your product. If someone purchases a product from you and later needs customer service, that service must be at the same level to maintain their previous positive experience when buying the product. Too often, I've seen more emphasis on the product and less on customer service. This can completely taint a customer's view of the brand. It becomes clear when a company hasn't given the same level of attention to anything outside the product itself. If a customer encounters an issue and struggles with warranty service, phone support, or even lodging a complaint, that experience shapes their overall perception of the brand.

Some companies today don't even offer phone support, and their email support is lacking. Making it easy for customers to reach you is crucial. All of this contributes to the customer experience.

You should take every aspect seriously to ensure the same attention to detail across the board. One negative experience can impact a customer's overall impression of your product and brand. In some cases, they may even turn to a competitor or switch to a different product—not because they dislike your product, but because they had a negative experience. This can lead them to perceive your company as unreliable. They could also see themselves being at risk when issues arise with the products they purchased from you.

So, be intentional in ensuring that every interaction a customer has with your products, services, or brand is a positive experience—one that mirrors the excitement of bringing home an album you've been waiting for. Your goal should be to create that same level of engagement and loyalty for your brand.

Make it a priority in your company to ensure that all of these touch-points are positive for the customer. Listen to your customers and take small steps to gauge their reactions. If they don't react as you expected, you pivot—take a different approach or try something new to engage them. If you're striving to create a holistic experience, you have to be open to experimenting with different strategies.

Exercise: *Use three words to describe how you want your customers to feel when they engage with your product and support. And does your current product and support achieve that goal?*

In some cases, your customers may feel frustrated—which is obviously not your desired outcome. But by listening to your customers, reading reviews, and gathering feedback, as we discussed earlier, you should know how they feel. You also need to determine whether their experience aligns with what you originally intended when you created your product.

Every business has an idea of what they want their customers to experience. They believe their product will help improve lives, increase productivity, or bring value.

But sometimes, as I mentioned, what you think they're feeling is not what they're actually feeling. That's why it's crucial to assess customer sentiment and ensure that every interaction they have with your brand is positive.

The next step is to ask yourself if you're doing the research to confirm that your customers are having the experience you intended. If they're not, what three steps can you take to achieve your desired result?

How can you improve? Maybe it's refining your customer service, enhancing your warranty policy, or making adjustments to improve the overall customer experience.

Exercise: *What is your favorite album?*

We talked about the experience of buying albums and everything that made them special. So, what is your favorite album? The one you cherish the most—the one you consider your all-time favorite? What impact has it had on your life?

Some people love an album so much that they frame it and hang it on their wall. Whether it's because of the artwork, the associated memories, or something else, it becomes a meaningful part of their identity.

In the next chapter, we'll talk about finding new revenue streams for your products and developing trust in your brand. We also discuss leveraging social media and other channels to grow your audience and generate buzz for your brand.

14

PUBLISHING, TOURING, AND MERCH

One of the things that's really important for any business is to figure out how many ways they can monetize their core products. The obvious way is to build your product focused on a particular audience and then sell your product to that audience. There are also other ways to potentially market and monetize your products or create new products that can add additional revenue streams to your company. In the music context, when a band puts out an album, they also have other ways to make money.

Usually, when an artist signs with a label, they first record the music and then release it to the world. Then, they go out on tour as a way to promote the album they just released. In this case, they're making money from the album through whatever deal they made with the record label, but they're also making money from touring. They get paid for each live performance. This represents another way for the artist to monetize and make money off the music they've written and created. It can be a global tour to reach their fan base and bring in new fans. The live shows are produced to create amazing experiences for people who love their music.

After the show, they sell their merchandise. In an earlier chapter, we talked about capturing fans in the moment while they're still on a high from the show. Selling merch is certainly one way of doing that. I think people are most likely to part with their money when they're emotionally attached to an experience they enjoyed. They're still feeling bliss and whatever emotions they have when leaving the concert. They're excited, talking about how great it was and maybe recalling their favorite part of the show. They're proud to buy the merchandise because the band gave them such a wonderful experience. They're more than happy to buy the t-shirt and wear it and represent their affinity for that particular band or artist.

Ultimately, it's about building a culture. It creates a culture not only among you and your friends but also among anyone else who identifies with that band or show. You might meet people who attended the same concert, sharing stories about how wonderful it was. It's another way for bands to capture that emotion in the moment and make money from their merch.

But what other areas can bands make money from? Back in the day, before social media and digital music, it was truly about promoting music through radio, touring, and selling records at a store. But you also had publishing, which is really important. If you write your own songs and own the publishing rights, you can collect royalties based on how the underlying musical composition of your song is used—performances, sheet music, reproduction, etc. If you own the recording of the musical composition (the sound recording), you can collect royalties for its use, separate from the musical composition.

You can also get paid by licensing your music for use with visual media —otherwise known as sync licensing—such as television shows, movies, and commercials. If you're a songwriter, you can make money by licensing your music. However, if you're only performing the music and didn't write the underlying song—which happens more often than people realize—then most of your income comes from recording the songs and touring.

With platforms like Spotify, Apple Music, and Amazon Music, artists can collect royalties through streaming. Some artists are also successful in monetizing their music through social media engagement.

There are several ways a band can engage with their fans and generate multiple revenue streams. This engagement allows them to continuously monetize their music, even when they are not touring or releasing new music. Some artists generate revenue through brand partnerships, which also allows them to reach new fans. Brand partnerships are a great way for artists to connect with a global or targeted audience by attaching their celebrity to a product or service. It's not unusual to see a popular artist in a television commercial promoting a product or collaborating with a brand to sell products. I recently noticed collaborations between Post Malone and Oreo Cookies, as well as Megan Thee Stallion and Revlon.

Another way artists generate revenue is through fan experiences like meet and greets. These are usually VIP experiences where fans get to meet their favorite artists up close and personal. Some artists also do private shows, for which they are paid. These aren't typical concerts where tickets are made available to the public—it could be a wedding, a birthday party, or another special occasion.

Another way to create additional revenue streams is by building trust in your brand, which allows you to expand your product base. Using a business context, one example is Yeti. Yeti started with ice coolers—rugged, tough coolers built to last. I owned a Yeti cooler, and it was the best cooler I ever had. Built like a tank, but expensive. They have a great brand and have now expanded from coolers to a wide range of products. They've entered other product categories while maintaining their reputation for durability, toughness, and high-quality craftsmanship. This consistency is crucial for building trust with an audience. Once you build trust in your brand, customers are more likely to purchase new products from you based on that trust. If you're looking for a durable tumbler or a well-made sweater, you'll consider buying from a brand you already trust, even if it's not their core product.

Another example is Patagonia. Patagonia started with outdoor clothing—a great product from a strong brand. They built an amazing clothing business, and now they sell food. I don't know how many people know this, but if you check the canned fish section at the supermarket, you might see Patagonia's brand. It's a brilliant move because people who buy Patagonia clothing often spend time outdoors, hiking or camping. And they have to eat. So, if you trust Patagonia's clothing for its quality, you're more likely to trust their canned fish.

That trust is critical. Brands that successfully expand into other areas do so because they establish an emotional connection with consumers while maintaining the same consistency and quality found in their core products. However, customers get disappointed when they try multiple versions of a product, and some fall short of their expectations.

Be creative and think outside the box—as long as it aligns with your mission, values, and purpose while providing a consistent customer experience. If you follow these principles, you can successfully expand into other areas as well.

Using these examples as inspiration, consider how you can generate additional revenue streams for your business. Be creative with your team. We've discussed the importance of fostering a creative environment and encouraging the free flow of ideas. Make sure you support and promote this because you never know where the best idea will come from. At the end of the day, the goal is to bring the best product idea to life—and often, that idea might not be yours.

It could come from the people you're collaborating with—the people you've hired who know the product, the audience, and the customers. They might have even better ideas than you for bringing a solution to life. The key is to act on those ideas, as there may be other innovative ways to monetize your brand or product.

Maybe there are acquisition or joint venture opportunities. Perhaps you can license your technology or offer white-label versions of your product for other companies to sell under their own brand. Or you could create a different version of your product to sell in secondary markets, appealing to a new customer base. You can also explore brand partnerships to expand your reach and fan base.

There are countless ways to extend your brand presence or create new revenue streams. However, revenue streams may not be immediate. For instance, when entering a new market, it can take time to build your audience, but an investment today might yield profits in the future. Ensure you have a solid strategic plan in place when pursuing these new revenue paths. This allows you to evaluate ideas thoroughly, clarify roles, track progress, measure success, and hold everyone accountable.

Another way to generate revenue is by keeping your fans buzzing about your brand. Engagement is key. There's significant promotional activity when bands go on tour, just as when they release new music. But what about when they're not touring or releasing music? How do they stay relevant to their fans? How can they keep fans engaged and interested? Social media is the best way to do this today, especially with platforms like TikTok, Instagram, and Facebook. These platforms allow bands to maintain engagement and stay top of mind when fans want to stay connected.

The same applies to businesses. Some customers want to learn more about the companies behind the products they buy. What are the company's mission, values, and purpose? What are they doing to make the world a better place? Where are their products made? Are they sustainable and environmentally friendly? Through social media and other media outlets, companies can tell their story to familiarize customers with their products, strengthen their brand identity, and highlight their impact.

Companies should be creative in engaging with customers on social media and pay attention to how their audience responds. For example, some companies have never been on TikTok but decide: *Why not? Let's get on TikTok and give users a unique experience.* Customers get to interact with the brand in a new way and potentially have a positive experience.

Companies have an opportunity here to be truly creative. It's not always easy. When you're deeply involved in creating your product, it's easy to focus solely on how you originally intended to market it. But there are countless ways to present your brand to your audience in a fresh, engaging way while still aligning with your mission, values, and purpose —and it can be fun.

TikTok has unlocked the opportunity for creative potential for many companies. Some brands never expected to use the platform, but after seeing others go viral with fun and engaging content, they decided to experiment. Some TikTok videos work well; others don't. Some videos are silly, some are weird, and some are just plain fun. The important thing is that companies are willing to push boundaries and try new and creative ways to connect with their audiences.

I encourage companies to embrace creativity. However, with any marketing approach, you should always ask: *Is this true to our brand? Are we being authentic? Are we prioritizing the customer?* If the answer is yes to all three, you're on the right path to authentically engaging your audience and building stronger connections.

Businesses can also expand their reach by appearing on podcasts and participating in interviews. Identify podcasts relevant to your industry, connect with influential hosts, and use these platforms to discuss your products and services. Share stories about how your company makes a difference in people's lives.

Storytelling is essential. Talk about how customers use your products, how your brand has impacted their lives, and how your team prioritizes customer needs. And don't let it be just you, the leader, speaking—get others in your company involved. Encourage employees to share their experiences, and even invite customers to tell their own stories about how your products or customer service have made a difference for them.

Consider sponsorship opportunities as well. Brands often sponsor concerts, charity events, and other high-visibility occasions. Sponsoring or co-sponsoring an event can be a great way to increase brand awareness and keep your business in front of potential customers.

Make sure you inform your customers about new product launches, partnerships, awards, or other exciting developments through announce-ments and press releases. When bands have an upcoming album or tour, they announce it to their audience. Similarly, you can share milestones like reaching one million subscribers, winning an industry award, or part-nering with an artist to promote a new product.

Think creatively about how to engage your customers consistently. Highlight wins within your organization, new product releases, and posi-tive reviews or articles about your brand. Use these moments to keep fans excited about what you have to offer. Seek out media coverage, collabo-rate with the press, and be proactive in getting your message out.

If there are magazines, newspapers, online blogs, or other media outlets that align with your audience, reach out and offer to discuss your product and how it benefits their readers or listeners. You could include giveaways or promotional discounts to incentivize engagement and further grow your brand.

Industry conferences and events are also valuable opportunities. Try to secure a spot on a conference panel, be a keynote speaker, or even purchase a booth at an event. These settings allow you to meet customers in person, answer questions about your products, and strengthen your brand's connection with its audience.

Another powerful way to increase engagement and impact is through philanthropy. Sponsorships are one aspect, but giving back is an even more meaningful way to connect with your fans. Purpose is essential, and philanthropy allows you to live your values and demonstrate your commitment to making the world a better place.

Find nonprofit organizations that align with your mission, values, and goals. Engaging in philanthropy extends your brand's reach and shows your customers that you genuinely care and follow through on your commitments.

Community involvement also provides opportunities for your employees to engage. Encourage team members to volunteer at charitable events, participate in food or clothing drives during the holidays, or contribute to philanthropic initiatives throughout the year. Make philanthropy a core part of your company culture—it validates your purpose and reinforces your commitment to creating a positive impact. It's not just about the products and services you offer but also about the actions of the people within your organization. Your employees should be actively involved in initiatives reflecting your company's mission, values, and purpose.

Exercise: *Identify three additional revenue streams you can create with your products or services.*

Take the time to sit down and carefully think this through.

You may already have a strategic plan—perhaps a one-year, three-year, or five-year projection outlining upcoming product launches and business growth. However, if you haven't fully explored this yet or simply haven't had time, now is an excellent opportunity to brainstorm three additional revenue streams with your team. Encourage your team to contribute creative ideas. Lean on them—you never know what innovative solutions they might propose to generate additional revenue for your company.

Be creative. Think outside the box and even beyond your industry if your products have the potential to succeed in other markets.

Exercise: *What is your favorite concert t-shirt?*

I've been to some fantastic concerts over the years and have bought t-shirts along the way. Sometimes, I bought one just to support the band; other times, I bought it for the cool design. I think we all have that one favorite T-shirt. So what is yours? And what's the story behind it? What concert did you attend? What band was it? Take a moment to relive the experience—go back to that moment and think about why that t-shirt is your favorite and what significance it holds in your life.

With success often comes crises and chaos as companies deal with rapid growth. In the next chapter, we focus on providing insights to help leaders manage uncertainty by maintaining team chemistry and alignment. We also address stress and burnout in the workplace and how leaders can be proactive in mitigating their effects.

PART VIII
PILLAR EIGHT: MANAGING STARDOM

15

FROM GARAGES TO STADIUMS

*W*hen many bands first start out—especially garage bands—they aspire to be the best in whatever genre they pursue, whether rock, rap, or country. A band may form in high school, jamming in the garage in the afternoons, thinking they sound pretty good. They imagine making a career out of it. So they keep practicing and refining their sound, eventually playing small local clubs.

At first, they might have only ten fans in the audience. Then, the next time they play, twenty people show up. A few months later, there are over 100. Before long, they are playing for huge, sold-out crowds. That's the dream—to go from a small garage band performing for friends to playing in front of 30,000 strangers in a stadium.

Anyone who wants to be excellent in business should have the same mindset. You start by getting your product out there so people can try it. Once they try it, they like it and start buying it more regularly. They tell their friends, and suddenly, you're building a fan base. Instead of selling 100 units a week, now you're selling 1,000. Then 10,000. Then 20,000. And before you know it, things start taking off. You're on your way to success!

But getting there takes hard work. In music, artists often spend years practicing and playing local gigs before making it big. The key is working hard every day to improve—honing their skills, writing new music, and practicing with the hope of reaching stardom. It's a constant grind. They work as a team to refine their craft and push themselves individually to become better musicians—whether that means becoming a stronger drummer, a better bass player, or a more skilled guitarist.

So when the opportunity finally comes, they're ready to seize it. I can think of several artists who took full advantage of their breakthrough moment with a massive debut album—Hootie & the Blowfish with *Cracked Rear View*, Counting Crows with *August and Everything After*, and Alanis Morissette with *Jagged Little Pill*. These were all incredible albums that launched each artist into stardom. Another great example is Nirvana's *Nevermind*—a groundbreaking album that took a grunge band from Washington and turned them into an international phenomenon.

Other genres also had their share of breakthrough artists. One of my personal favorites was the hip-hop group De La Soul. I played their debut album, *Three Feet High and Rising*, on repeat when it came out. Another rap group from that era that remains a favorite of mine is A Tribe Called Quest, now inducted into the Rock & Roll Hall of Fame. Their debut album, *People's Instinctive Travels and the Paths of Rhythm*, is still in rotation on my playlist. I could name so many other groups from different genres and eras that achieved great success with their debut albums. But the common theme here is going from selling a few records to selling millions.

In business, you want to experience the same kind of growth—going from selling 10 products to 1,000 and then one million. From five customers to five million. That's the goal of anyone in business, whether you're selling products, gaining clicks on YouTube, or growing an audience on TikTok or Instagram. It's all about expanding your reach and building a fan base.

But managing that growth can be challenging. You may not have the resources or infrastructure to scale appropriately. For example, if you're a software company and a TikTok video about your product goes viral, tens of thousands of people may suddenly flood your website to download it. If your servers can't handle the traffic, your system could crash. As you scale, you not only have to manage your company's resources and infrastructure, but you also have to manage your team—which is arguably the most challenging part of managing rapid growth.

When you go from a small operation to being the hottest product on the market, you have to be prepared for everything that comes with it. Everybody wants to buy it. Everybody wants to interview you and talk to you. And suddenly, you realize you have far more responsibility than before.

One of the biggest challenges is hiring quickly. When demand skyrockets, you often need more people to meet it. But how do you scale your team while maintaining the chemistry and culture of your organization? When hiring rapidly, you may not be as diligent in ensuring that new hires align with your mission, values, and purpose.

You might not have time to thoroughly evaluate whether they're the right fit for the role or your team dynamic. As your company grows, you find yourself surrounded by new people you don't know well. You've spent time building a strong team, but with so many new hires, you simply don't have the capacity anymore to personally connect with everyone. You still have to run the company and manage the increasing external demands on your time.

Suddenly, more people want to interview you. More people want to engage with you. Your responsibilities as a leader multiply, and you must balance them all. You also need to coordinate with external resources—third-party contractors, vendors, advertising agencies, and others.

As your company scales, it becomes increasingly difficult to thoroughly vet everyone. You want to grow quickly, but sometimes you can't control how fast that growth happens. So, how do you ensure that new hires and external partners align with your vision? How do you maintain the integrity of your business while scaling at an unpredictable pace?

This is one of the most significant challenges leaders face. When managing chaos and growth, staying true to your mission, values, and purpose is key. These should be your guiding principles that you measure every decision, new hire, and partnership against. Maintaining this alignment will help you navigate rapid expansion while preserving the core of what made your business successful in the first place.

Your strategic objectives and goals must align with your company's mission, values, and purpose. As demands increase, as you hire outside companies, and as you respond to requests for interviews, articles, and other obligations, you have to stay grounded in what got you there. Rely on those principles moving forward because your vision can quickly become clouded by the sheer volume of things you now have to manage. At times, it can feel like drinking from a firehose.

Managing this level of growth is incredibly challenging. Not only must you stay aligned with your mission, values, and purpose, but your executive team must also. This is the time when appropriate delegation becomes essential.

You have to trust your team. As their leader, you have to believe that you have instilled in them the skills and knowledge they need to help manage growth.

Too often, leaders try to shoulder everything themselves. But you quickly realize that's not sustainable. You must rely on the people around you, which is why building strong team chemistry is critical. That's why we previously emphasized practice, practice, practice—getting to know your teammates personally and professionally, understanding their strengths and weaknesses, so when times get tough, you'll know exactly who to turn to for what. You'll understand what can be accomplished together and recognize when you need external support.

Sometimes, you may find that your team doesn't have the internal expertise to handle a particular challenge. In those cases, you'll need to hire an outside vendor or company to help navigate the situation. But even then, you must ensure that any external partners align with your mission, values, and purpose. Their contributions should reinforce the customer connection you want to maintain.

Everything about your brand matters—your image, your messaging, and the emotional attachment you create with customers. It's similar to how a band cultivates an emotional connection with its fans. You need to preserve that connection in everything you do.

The music remains the same, even if you go from being a garage band to selling out stadiums.

The way you played that song in front of five friends should be the same way you play it in front of 30,000 people. Sure, you might have bigger amplifiers, fancier guitars, and a road crew—but at the end of the day, the customer experience should remain consistent. Maintain that authenticity as you grow.

Amazon started in a garage in 1994, selling books online. Of course, they were small at the time, but one thing Jeff Bezos instilled in his team was a "customer-centric" approach. We've talked about the importance of establishing your mission, values, and purpose as a guiding light for your business. Amazon's guiding principle was customer-centricity—everything revolved around the customer. Seeing how that approach shaped the company into what it is today is incredible.

One example of their customer-first approach was making purchasing a product as easy as possible. They developed the "one-click" feature, allowing customers to buy a book with a single click. They even patented the technology. Another example is their focus on expedited delivery. They've refined the process to the point where, in some cases, you can order a product and receive it the same day.

This customer-centric approach also aids decision-making. When a company is scaling rapidly, you and your team must make quick decisions. Do your core principles help guide those decisions? If your team consistently follows a customer-first mindset, it allows them to make decisions more effectively—always keeping the customer's needs at the forefront.

And that's what drives their decision-making—doing what they need to for the betterment of the company. It becomes much easier to manage chaos when your team is in sync. If your team lacks direction and doesn't fully understand the company's mission, values, or purpose, it can lead to even more chaos.

Imagine a programmer on your team is writing code to add new features to your product, but they don't know how their work aligns with the company's goals and objectives. That uncertainty can make it difficult for them to make quick, informed decisions that benefit the overall product. Without proper leadership, they may struggle to make the right calls in the moment, potentially leading to poor decision-making that affects product quality. That's why it's crucial to ensure everyone is aligned—so you can navigate chaos together and make micro-decisions that keep you on track for growth.

Another major challenge of scaling and managing chaos is dealing with stress and burnout. That's inevitable. I've seen many companies—especially startups—try to compensate by increasing the workload of existing employees rather than hiring additional staff. I understand why; I've been a part of startups myself. But the danger is that you can easily overwork your team. And remember, they trust you.

As a leader, your role isn't just to delegate tasks and challenge your team to grow—it's also to protect them when they're overwhelmed, stressed, or burnt out. Sometimes, you need to step in and say, "Take the day off. I think you're working too hard. Take the weekend to decompress." Maybe offer extra vacation days.

As a leader, you have control over how to manage workloads and prevent burnout. The key is to stay actively engaged, listen to your team, and be aware of the stress levels within your organization—just as we talked about with bands. You need to hear when there's a problem and recognize the presence of burnout.

Stay connected with your team. Make sure everyone is in sync. If one team member is struggling—like a drummer falling behind in a band—step in and encourage the rest of the team to support them. Work together to lift each other up.

That's absolutely critical. One way to be proactive as a leader is by setting realistic work expectations. If you see a team member working until midnight every night, you know that's unhealthy and unsustainable. You have to find solutions to prevent that. Maybe you can add someone to the team to lighten the workload. You can also offer flexible working arrangements.

For example, if a team member is dealing with personal matters, allow them to work from home for a few days. Trust here is essential. If employees are working remotely, you need to have confidence in them. Even if you're not physically present, you should trust that they maintain the same level of performance and professionalism—staying aligned with the company's mission, values, and purpose.

You want to balance the workload across the team. If one person is overworked while others have lighter workloads, find ways to redistribute tasks or encourage teamwork to complete assignments more efficiently. Be proactive in fostering a team-oriented mindset by enabling your team to step in when they see a colleague struggling. If someone has finished their tasks and notices a teammate needs help, they should feel empowered to offer assistance.

It shouldn't be a situation where people think, *Well, that's not my job* or *They can handle it themselves.* What truly makes teams cohesive is when members support and uplift one another. At the end of the day, you're all working toward a shared goal.

Success is achieved collectively—as a team and as a company. No single person can do it alone. The best teams, the ones that win, and the bands that succeed are those that take care of each other. Make sure you foster that culture.

Look out for one another. Everyone has good days and bad days. Support each other through the tough times and celebrate wins together when things go well.

You also need to scale your team when necessary. If the workload becomes too much, consider hiring additional staff, bringing in independent contractors, or partnering with a third-party agency to help manage the load. This is especially important when scaling a business, navigating chaos, or managing rapid growth.

As a leader, you should also encourage healthy boundaries. Let your team know that work calls and emails are discouraged on weekends. If you feel compelled to send an email outside work hours, clarify that an immediate response isn't required. For example, you might say, "We can discuss this on Monday. No need to respond now—I just wanted to get my thoughts down."

Maintaining effective communication and feedback is critical. Make sure communication channels are open during the workweek so you can identify burnout, stress, or workload concerns before they escalate. You want to hear directly from your team when issues arise—not through secondhand reports or after it's too late to prevent a bigger problem. Just like a band needs to stay in tune, your team must stay aligned and connected. Ensuring that everyone is on the same page is crucial for long-term success.

Another way to manage stress and prevent burnout is by establishing effective time management strategies. Good time management allows your team to operate efficiently, accomplishing more without increasing stress levels or leading to exhaustion. As a leader, you must take a proactive approach to time management. The first step is conducting a time audit—identify tasks or processes within your organization that waste time or hinder productivity. Look for inefficiencies that prevent you and your team from performing at a high level. You can free up time and create a more productive, less stressful work environment by eliminating these obstacles.

One area of focus for a time audit should be reducing or eliminating unnecessary meetings. Meetings can be some of the biggest time wasters. Sometimes, we attend recurring meetings simply because they are on the calendar. Over time, we may realize they are not only unproductive but also taking time away from more valuable work. As a leader, be intentional about meetings. Establish a framework to ensure that every meeting provides value, and eliminate those that are unnecessary or could be handled through a quick phone call, a one-on-one discussion, or another more efficient method. For example, preparation before meetings is required, meetings must have reasonable time limits, and individuals get a finite amount of time to speak on specific topics. I've been in meetings where people talk endlessly without adding value or reaching solutions. Implementing meeting guidelines will maximize efficiency and reduce time spent away from more productive tasks.

Also, empower your team to decline unnecessary meetings and leave meetings early once they've contributed their portion. Encourage feedback on how to make meetings more efficient and productive. Emails can also be time wasters. A quick phone call can often resolve an issue more efficiently than a long back-and-forth email chain.

Disorganization is another major time drain. Searching for a misplaced file, document, or note can take thirty minutes—30 minutes wasted. Implementing a standardized filing system where employees can quickly access necessary information will improve efficiency. As a leader, provide your team with the resources they need to stay organized and perform optimally.

Lack of planning is another time-waster. If you don't plan ahead, you may waste time correcting avoidable mistakes or redoing careless work. Even worse, your lack of planning may create unnecessary fire drills for your co-workers, which can significantly impact team chemistry. Have you ever heard the famous Bob Carter quote: "Poor planning on your part does not necessitate an emergency on mine"?

Micromanaging should also be minimized or eliminated. If a team member requires extra guidance, provide proper training or assign them a mentor rather than micromanaging their every move. Understanding your team's strengths and weaknesses allows you to build trust and delegate tasks more effectively.

Multitasking is another common but misleading time waster. Many of us believe we can handle ten things at once efficiently, but in reality, we can't. Constantly switching between tasks reduces focus, and when you return to a task after being distracted, you may lose continuity of thought, making it harder to complete the task effectively. I encourage leaders to block time for high-priority tasks. Identify your most important tasks and work on them first. Set aside dedicated time to focus on these tasks without interruptions. Constantly shifting attention from one task to another makes it difficult to complete anything efficiently, often resulting in lower-quality work.

Delegation is also key for a leader. If you can easily assign a task to someone else and they can complete it promptly, delegate it. Before delegating, communicate clearly with the person taking on the task to ensure mutual understanding of expectations, deadlines, and deliverables. Being able to delegate effectively frees up your time to focus on higher-priority responsibilities.

Once you've developed a framework for time management, make sure you communicate it clearly to your team. For example, if you empower people to leave meetings early or remove themselves from meeting lists, everyone should be aware of this policy. This prevents any misunderstanding or awkwardness when someone gets up and walks out of a meeting. The remaining participants will understand that the person leaving has other high-priority tasks to focus on. As a leader, it's important to establish these rules to ensure there are no issues when people try to work more efficiently and prioritize their time effectively.

Another key aspect of leadership is celebrating your team's accomplishments. Recognize the wins. It's important to create moments where you tell your team, "Great job!" and let them share in the joy of the achievement. It's also an opportunity to discuss what the team did well and gather feedback on areas for improvement. Learning from challenges strengthens team chemistry and prepares everyone for the next project.

As a leader, your role is to help your team succeed. You want every individual to thrive, and it's your job to support their success in every way possible. Because guess what? If they succeed, you succeed. If they fail, you fail. So don't ever approach leadership with an "it's all on me" mentality. Yes, the responsibility falls on you, but you'll make a much greater impact by working collectively with your team rather than trying to shoulder everything alone.

> **Exercise:** *Create a checklist with three steps you would take to manage crisis and chaos and three steps you would take to reduce stress and burnout in your organization as it grows.*

This is important because it prepares you before a crisis occurs. Think of it this way: if you're a pilot, you want to have a checklist ready for emergencies. If turbulence hits, you should already know the three steps you will take to get through it.

It's better to plan ahead when your mind is clear rather than scrambling to figure it out during a crisis. It's like creating a disaster kit before an emergency happens—you wouldn't want to assemble a survival kit *while* in the middle of a disaster.

Keep this checklist readily available and refer to it regularly. As things move faster, this preparation will ensure you're ready to take action and lead your team effectively when the time comes.

In times of chaos or crisis, clear and consistent messaging is essential. You will need to communicate with your team—letting them know what's happening, how you plan to manage it, and what steps you will take to pivot or resolve the issue.

Communication is critical. I emphasize this throughout the book because if there's one key takeaway, it's this: *Effective communication and feedback between you and your team are essential for your organization to grow from the garage to the stadium.*

Exercise: *List five songs that help you get through stress and burnout—songs that lift you up no matter how tough things get.*

Play them on repeat when you need motivation and resilience. Feel free to add more songs over time. This is your playlist, and you control what goes on it.

In the next chapter, we'll explore how companies can effectively scale their organizations through strategic planning and enhance team chemistry through effective collaboration. It's important to have the right plan and people in place to build cohesion and sustainability.

16

SCALES, CHORDS, AND
SUSTAINABILITY

*I*f you don't have a strategic plan to manage growth, now is the time to create one. We discussed managing crisis and chaos in the previous chapter, and part of handling success is navigating those challenges by relying on your mission, values, and purpose while ensuring everyone is aligned. That's one approach, but having a solid plan is just as crucial. A strategic plan will help you scale your organization and provide a structured framework for your team.

If you don't have a plan or haven't prepared for what's ahead, you're setting yourself up for failure. Some companies have a strategic plan, but they don't execute it. They may have hired a third party to create an impressive-looking document, but they never actually follow it. I always say that if you have a strategic plan but don't follow it, then you don't have a strategic plan at all.

If you have a strategic plan, make sure it's one you will *actually* use. That's why involving your executive team in its creation is important. Ensure that everyone is on board and understands each part of the plan, including their roles and responsibilities in executing the plan.

A strong strategic plan will guide your growth and provide the structure needed to keep everyone aligned. Think of it like a band scaling from garages to stadiums—growth requires a team, and as the band becomes more successful, that team expands.

They have a manager. They might have an agent. They have an attorney. They work with people from their label.

As the team grows, there is a clear structure in place. Managers and labels understand this structure because they've worked with other bands and artists who have experienced similar levels of success.

They know exactly what's needed:

- Who to hire to book venues
- Who to bring in for road crew support
- Who to hire for marketing and advertising
- Who will design and produce tour merchandise
- Which trucking companies will transport equipment
- Which technicians to hire to ensure instruments, amplifiers, and sound systems function properly

There is a system in place to support success. Similarly, in business, having a strategic plan means knowing what roles and resources are necessary at each stage of growth. Without that structure, scaling effectively becomes much more challenging.

All of these elements form a structured system—knowing what needs to be done and when, and who is responsible for doing it. Once the band goes on tour, they don't have to worry about these details. They just need to know where and when to show up. That structure is essential because if the band had to manage all of it themselves, they'd have no time to focus on the music itself.

The band primarily focuses on the music and their performance. But can they successfully book Madison Square Garden for a gig without help? Maybe, but usually, that's handled by professionals on their team who specialize in booking venues of that scale.

When I played in cover bands back in the day, we booked our own shows. We'd call up venues and say, "Hey, we'd like to perform there." We'd introduce ourselves and sometimes send a tape so they could hear what we sounded like. But when you're transitioning from garages to stadiums, you let the professionals handle it.

Stadiums need to be booked well in advance. Deposits have to be paid, equipment has to be reserved, and every logistical detail must be managed to ensure a seamless event. The goal is to provide the best possible experience for the fans.

Everything matters—from ticket sales and ease of access to ensuring the venue is clean, the lighting correct, and the sound perfect. When the audience arrives, they should be able to enjoy the show without distractions. These elements are all part of the structure supporting the band's growth.

So when a band moves from a garage to a stadium, the music remains the same, but the experience changes—bigger stages, more lights, better sound. However, the *emotional connection* between the audience and the artist stays the same. In some cases, it can even be elevated with the added production elements that a larger venue allows.

For companies, having a plan provides that same structure. A strategic plan is the best way to achieve this. It should include your mission and values, which we've already discussed, as well as your vision for the company. It may also include a **SWOT analysis**—an assessment of your **Strengths, Weaknesses, Opportunities, and Threats**.

- **Strengths** include the quality of your product, the expertise of your team, or a strong customer base.
- **Weaknesses** might be limited resources, lack of market share, or challenges in distribution.
- **Opportunities** could come from new regulations that favor your product, emerging partnerships, or untapped markets where you can sell or bundle your products to create additional revenue streams.
- **Threats** include economic uncertainty, rising costs, new regulations affecting your industry, or competitors with more advanced products entering the market.

A SWOT analysis helps you anticipate challenges and develop strategies to maintain market share and retain customers.

It's also essential to analyze your industry regularly. Always keep an eye on what's happening in your market. Track emerging competitors, observe who is entering or exiting the industry, and pay attention to market trends. These trends could be driven by shifts in customer demand, economic factors, or technological advancements. By staying informed and prepared, you position yourself for long-term success.

A great example of that is AI. Now that companies utilize AI, the landscape of how your particular product will compete in that industry could change. Whether or not you decide to use AI, how does its evolution impact your business? If your competitors are using it to gain an advantage, you have to determine if you want to use it.

You balance that with other factors, such as privacy. Some people are unsure about AI and its impact on privacy. But again, as a leader, you have to navigate that and have a strategic plan for how you will address technological innovations and adopt them within your company to improve your product and customer experience while balancing their impact on privacy. All of that has to factor into the industry overview, your goals, and your objectives. What do you want to accomplish? Remember to use the SMART goals framework discussed earlier in the book.

If you haven't already, this is a great time to plan what your company wants to achieve in one, three, and five years. It's not necessarily just about money. Of course, you want your company to make [X] number of dollars in three years or [X] number of dollars in five years. But how do you get there? What are the goals? What are the milestones? What does success look like at each milestone? What new products do you have to release, or what changes or upgrades to your existing products or services will help you reach your goals? That's where the strategic plan comes in. You need to identify those strategic initiatives and have a plan for achieving them as a team.

You should also include a marketing plan. When your company creates new products or adds features or improvements to existing products, do you have a plan to market them? How can you generate buzz and interest in these new products or improvements? How do you keep your customers happy and give them what they want?

You should also include an operational plan. What changes do you have to make internally in your organization to support growth? You may need to expand your accounting department, bring on more personnel in your technology group, or add more attorneys to your legal team because of new regulations sweeping through your industry.

Adding financial projections to your strategic plan is also essential. How will your new products or improvements impact revenue and profits over time? What will your costs be to execute your strategic plan? Create financial projections to see how that will impact your growth and how your organization will scale from a financial standpoint.

You also want to examine key roles and responsibilities to understand the personnel needed to execute the plan. This is vital. You can create the best strategic plan ever, with beautiful graphs and charts, but if you don't execute it effectively, you will not achieve your goals and objectives as a company. So you need to identify the roles necessary to accomplish the tasks that will meet those goals and objectives. Some roles may already exist in your company, but there may be new roles and people you need to add to execute the strategic plan.

You also need to assign those roles to the specific tasks at hand. It could be an individual or a team, depending on the need. You also need to clearly define the responsibilities associated with each role to accomplish your goals and objectives.

You also want to look at key performance indicators (KPIs). These are ways to measure your growth and ensure that everyone is on the right track to meet your goals and objectives. Additionally, you should establish action items for each role and each step along the way, identifying specific tasks that need to be completed at each stage of your growth.

You want to clarify what each person has to do and when they have to do it. Creating a timeline for monitoring progress will help you do that. I'm very visual, as are many other people, so you want to have a visual timeline where you and others on your team can see what you've done to date and where you need to go from a visual standpoint. You can see the tasks that need to be accomplished, who is assigned to them, and whether they have been completed. As team members accomplish their tasks, they are checked off.

The timeline is a visual way of making sure everybody stays on track and remains accountable. Everybody can see where they are and what needs to be done to accomplish the task. You can also see where someone might need help, so you can assign members of your team to pitch in as needed to keep everyone on track.

Once you have your strategic plan in place, you also want to focus on maintaining your team chemistry. As your organization grows, new people and moving parts can disrupt the chemistry you built with your initial team. But as a leader, you want to listen for these disruptions and act quickly to fix them.

Think about it like playing a chord on a guitar. A chord is a group of notes played together. It's powerful when you first learn to play a chord on a guitar. It doesn't sound all that great if you just strum the open strings. But if you form a chord and strum the strings, it can sound beautiful.

When I first learned to play a chord on a guitar, I was hooked. I think the D chord was the first chord I learned to play. And when you play those notes together—A, D, and F#—in that particular configuration, it makes a beautiful sound. If you were to pick three random notes on a guitar and just play them, it wouldn't sound great. But when you create a D chord, a G chord, or an A chord, now it sounds like something—and it sounds amazing. All the notes are now playing in harmony, and that's what creates the beautiful sound.

So how do you replicate that as you scale your organization? Ultimately, you want your team to operate like a chord. No matter how fast you grow, your team should stay in tune and remain harmonious. If things become disorganized and chaotic, you'll start hearing a different sound from your team—like playing all of the strings open on a guitar or playing random notes together. You can immediately hear that something is off—something abstract or not pleasing to the ear. So keep that chemistry alive through alignment with core principles, effective communication and feedback, a realistic and actionable strategic plan, and productive collaboration. That's how you want to look at your organization as you scale.

When you go from playing in front of three friends in your garage to 30,000 fans in a stadium, the level of anxiety goes way up. You now need to rely on each other more than ever to perform at a high level for each show. Maintaining team chemistry to sustain performance during tough and chaotic times can be difficult. It's important to lean on your core principles. As a leader, you always want to be in tune with what the team is doing. As the organization scales, you need to manage anxiety levels and control the chaos.

You want to make sure each member of your team is playing the right note to create a beautiful-sounding chord. That's the collaboration and cohesion part of it. If each person on your team is doing what they're supposed to be doing, you'll always have a beautiful chord. You'll always be in sync. You'll always be harmonious. And that will ensure that everything flows seamlessly as you scale.

The second you hear an off note, a note that's out of tune, or a note that is mistimed, that's when, as a leader, you need to step in and do what you can to improve the cohesion within your team. That may involve talking to each team member and figuring out where the issue lies—why the team is not cohesive. Communication and feedback are crucial here. If someone on your team is struggling or having issues, that's when you need to step in and say, "Okay, what can we do as a company to help you overcome these challenges you're facing right now?" Timing is very important when addressing these issues.

Timing is just as critical in leadership as it is in music. You want to listen and react as quickly as possible. You also want to empower your team to support one another. This is extremely important. I mentioned this in the last chapter, but I can't emphasize it enough. Not only should you be listening for when the team is out of sync, or something is going wrong, but your teammates should also be listening.

If you're the drummer in a band and you hear the bass player hit a wrong note or fall behind in timing, you want to empower the drummer to say something to the bass player. You want to create a culture where team members feel comfortable saying, "Hey, I think we're a little off here." However, the way you communicate is critical.

As a leader, you should be proactive in helping your team communicate effectively. Everyone has different personalities and quirks, but communication should encourage a positive response rather than a negative one. Team members should engage in active listening without being overly critical or defensive. Constant defensiveness only leads to more negative feedback. Instead, they should be able to accept constructive criticism to keep things moving forward and ensure the team stays on the right path.

Exercise: *Draft a three-paragraph statement you would send to your team to keep them focused, collaborative, and motivated as your organization scales.*

It's much easier to create a plan when things are going well rather than when you're already managing chaos. Take the time now, while things are stable, to prepare a statement that you can send to your team during challenging times. With a clear mind, you can thoughtfully craft a message that will bring them back to center and keep them aligned with your organization's mission, values, and purpose.

Exercise: *List five songs that would help motivate your team and bring them together during times of crisis and chaos.*

This should be a fun exercise because it gives you a chance to go through your playlist with a focus on what will help your team push through difficult moments.

You know your team. You know their personalities, what they like and don't like, what motivates them, and their strengths and weaknesses. Based on this knowledge, now is the time to create a playlist to help them navigate crisis and chaos.

In your mind, this playlist should restore harmony, energize them, inspire them, and motivate them to overcome whatever challenges they face. As a leader, you should have an idea of what songs might help them get back on track. Good luck!

In the next chapter, we'll explore the importance of reinforcing core principles as the foundation of your company's culture. Having a soundtrack for your organization that plays on repeat means everyone knows what guides them, what shapes their decision-making, and how they treat and interact with others.

PART IX
PILLAR NINE: PLAY ON REPEAT —THE SOUNDTRACK OF YOUR CULTURE

17

DEFINING YOUR SOUNDTRACK

*I*n this book, we've talked a lot about the evolution of a band and how it corresponds to the evolution of a business. An important theme throughout this book is sticking to your core principles —using them to build your team and business and leaning on them through crises and chaos. That's really important in everything we've discussed, from the moment you first decide to start a band to hopefully managing your enormous success.

You start by saying, "Okay, this is our mission—to be the best rock band we can be. These are the instruments we're going to play and the types of songs we're going to perform, and this is what makes us unique or different." But beyond that, you establish your mission, the values you will adhere to as a group, and your purpose—your why.

Then, you commit to working hard and collaborating as a team to achieve your goal—to be the best rock band in the world. The importance of maintaining consistency and continuity cannot be overstated: how you treat each other, how you react to challenges, how you interact with your audience and fans, how you think, how you make decisions, and how those decisions impact the band itself. All of that should align with your core principles as a band.

Those core principles are the glue that keeps everything together, even if you go from being a garage band to a stadium band. You want to constantly reinforce these principles and play them on repeat, which is one of the most important aspects of all of this.

Some businesses develop a strategic plan or outline how to execute a particular project. But once they have that plan, they put it on a shelf and don't follow it, or they go off script and ignore the carefully thought-out strategies they initially agreed upon. There's nothing inherently wrong with pivoting or adjusting your plan—companies must do that to stay ahead of the competition. You need the flexibility to make changes and adapt as a team as you move forward, and that's perfectly fine.

However, you also want to maintain consistency in your messaging so that everything still aligns with what the band—or company—has committed to. That includes your values, mission, and purpose. So, "play on repeat" means reinforcing these principles with everyone on the team, including any new members who join. This is important because you want these principles to be ingrained in their minds. It's one thing to know your mission, values, and purpose—it's another to live them truly.

And what's the beauty of music? The beauty of music is that when you hear a song repeatedly—even if it's just background noise in an elevator or a store—you end up knowing every lyric and every note. You might not even realize it initially, but the repetition makes the song stick. You could hear it a hundred times, and suddenly, you can sing the whole thing yourself. Maybe not well, but you can sing it. That's the power of playing a song on repeat.

You get to the point where you know every detail of the song and its nuances. You know precisely when the guitar solo is coming. You know when the lead singer belts out that first note. You know when that drumbeat hits. Earlier, I mentioned the song "In the Air Tonight" by Genesis, which is such a great song. When that powerful drum riff starts mid-song, you know exactly when it will happen. You might even stop what you're doing and play the drum riff in the air—I've certainly done it a few times.

Having a soundtrack for your organization that plays on repeat means everyone knows what guides them, what shapes their decision-making, and how they treat and interact with others. It becomes much easier to stay aligned and to manage through chaos and crisis because you are living your values, mission, and purpose. By doing that, it becomes easier to react when you need to make a decision with a customer or a vendor that impacts the company. You already know your principles.

You already know what you're going to do and how those principles influence your decision to ensure you make the right choice in a given situation. This is the importance of playing on repeat and having it be the soundtrack of your culture—you want your team to constantly hear the same message, to all be singing the same song.

When you are focused, aligned, and synchronized, you can get through anything together as a team. You know what each person is thinking and doing, and you make decisions collectively for the good of the group, helping to accomplish its goals and objectives. This is why it's important to have soundtracks that reinforce these principles—not only for those already in the organization but also for new hires, so they receive the same reinforcement.

Once you have established your mission, values, and purpose, there are many ways to continue reinforcing them. You can talk about them in meetings, whether they are one-on-one discussions or group meetings. You can reference them when making key decisions. For example, if a team member suggests, "Hey, I think we should do this deal," someone should speak up and ask, "Does this align with our mission, values, and purpose? If so, how?" These should be the questions driving decision-making within your organization. If everyone is asking these questions and living by these principles, the entire team will be on the same page regarding which deals to pursue, what improvements to make to products, how to respond to customers in the moment, and more. Your mission, values, and purpose influence everything in your organization—from how you make decisions to how you respond to and interact with people inside and outside your group.

The other important part is consistent management. As I said previously, you want to make sure that everyone on your team is aligned with the same soundtrack. If a certain song is added to the soundtrack but doesn't fit, it can affect the listening experience of the group.

An example of this in a musical context is if you're in a country band and the drummer says, "Hey, I have this wonderful jazz song I'd love to add to our playlist." The other band members would probably look at the drummer and say, "That doesn't align with our mission, values, and purpose. Why would we do a jazz song?" In that instance, it wouldn't make sense. The same concept applies to your company.

If you have established core principles, values, and a mission, you don't want to introduce something that contradicts them. You don't want someone operating under a different set of values and working based on their own system rather than the values the organization has agreed upon. You need to be aware of that.

Part of living the mission, values, and purpose as an organization is ensuring that your employees are aligned with them. This helps prevent alternative ideas that might steer the company away from its core principles. This is also why listening is so important. If your team hears something that isn't aligned with the group, they can act on it or at least bring it to your attention before it gets too far out of tune. They might say, "Hey, I'm hearing people talk about something that doesn't align with our core principles."

To be clear, I'm not encouraging people to snitch on their coworkers. My point is that it's important for your team to make sure everyone is singing the same tune. If they hear someone who isn't, they should address it. As a leader, you can empower them to talk to that person and say, "Look, I overheard you saying this, and I'm not sure it aligns with our mission, values, and purpose. Why do you think that's a good idea?" This way, you're encouraging them to coach in the moment and help bring people back on board in a positive way.

In my experience, positive reinforcement has always been a more effective way to help people understand and align with a mission than negative reinforcement or criticism. You want to encourage a free flow of ideas and communication, and the best way to do that is to ensure that everyone feels they can speak up for the betterment of the organization. So, make sure everyone on your team is listening to and aligned with the same soundtrack.

And remember, as you add new members to the group, ensure they are also aligned. If they want to add a new song to the soundtrack, it should fit. That will help ensure that your team is always listening to the same soundtrack, that all team members are reinforcing it, and that it's playing on repeat. This way, they are constantly reminded of the company's values, mission, and purpose, keeping everyone in tune.

> **Exercise:** *Create a five-song soundtrack that reflects the core principles of your culture.*

Do these songs reflect your organization's culture or the culture you aspire to create? Does the soundtrack reinforce your mission, values, and purpose? A soundtrack is important because it aligns, motivates, inspires, and reflects your culture. That's what you want to ensure. Once you create this five-song soundtrack, discuss it with your team and get their feedback. It's a great team-building exercise. Ask if they have songs that might better represent the core principles of your culture and why they feel that way. Once you agree on the soundtrack as a team, encourage them to play those songs on repeat as a reminder of what makes their culture special.

In this chapter, we focused on defining the soundtrack for your culture. The next chapter focuses on how leaders and their teams can incorporate that soundtrack into their daily lives. Keeping the soundtrack alive through repetition and reinforcement helps teams maintain consistency and alignment as your company grows.

18

LIVING THE SOUNDTRACK

*I*n Chapter 17, we talked about defining the fundamental elements of your soundtrack. This chapter focuses on embedding those core cultural principles into the daily operation of your group and leadership practices. Communication is key, as we've discussed throughout this book. It is a common theme because communication and feedback are critical for everyone to truly live the soundtrack.

You want to make sure that everyone on your team knows the soundtrack and lives it daily—in their work, decision-making, interactions with others in the group, and how they represent the team publicly. New hires should hear the soundtrack on day one and start living it from the beginning. You can also create visual representations to reinforce the soundtrack—something they see daily, just like listening to music every day.

For example, you might have signs, symbols, placards, digital wallpapers for computers, t-shirts, or coffee mugs featuring colors and messaging that align with your soundtrack. These elements help employees see and engage with the soundtrack every day. Maybe you display a sign in the coffee room or break area, or perhaps your company's values are listed on a board at the entrance so that employees see them as they walk in and out.

Some companies even place their values near the reception area, ensuring that customers, clients, or business partners see them when they visit. This can be very impactful because it demonstrates that you have values and have taken the time to define what's important. Additionally, these values often resonate with companies that want to do business with you, customers who buy your products, or people who interact with your brand. When others see that your company has clearly defined values that you actively adhere to, it can also strengthen your negotiation position. During discussions, you can reference these values by saying, "These are our values, and they must be reflected in the agreement." If your values are already well-established, championing them in negotiations becomes much easier.

Another benefit is that when every department follows the same values, it ensures consistency in decision-making and alignment across the organization. You can also reinforce this culture of alignment through leadership activities such as executive retreats, workshops, and seminars. For example, you might hold workshops focusing on your mission, values, and purpose, ensuring everyone is aligned.

These types of exercises can also be valuable for onboarding new hires. When new employees join your company, you could have them participate in a brief workshop or seminar where they answer questions or complete activities reinforcing the organization's mission, values, and purpose. This ensures that they understand the company's core messaging and expectations from day one. By embedding these principles early, new employees will have a clear sense of how to make decisions, interact with coworkers, and uphold company values.

Another great aspect of this approach is that if you bring on someone who, at first, seemed like a good fit during the hiring process but later appears misaligned with the company's core principles, they will see first-hand how others adhere to those principles. When they witness that these values are more than just words on a poster, that their colleagues are actively practicing them, it can influence them. They might think, *Wow, this really is the standard. People here actually live by these principles.* That realization makes it easier for them to adapt and say, *You know what, I should buy into this.* Maybe they were skeptical initially, but now they see everyone working in unison, aligned in their efforts to improve the company. It then becomes easier for them to get on board, fall in line, and start following the principles on their own.

On the flip side, they may decide, *This is not for me. These values don't work for me.* Then, it becomes clearer why they may not be the right fit. They will see the bar that has been set, understand the principles the company adheres to, and recognize whether they fit in or not. If they aren't willing to make the effort to align with those principles, then as a leader, you might need to make a tough decision. Personally, I always like to give people the opportunity to adjust. You point out the issues, give them a chance to improve, and allow them time to align with the company's values. But there may come a point where it becomes clear that they are simply not the right fit. If it's evident that they will never align with the core principles, it may make sense to part ways. Keeping them may do more harm than good if they are not contributing to the organization's growth and cohesion.

This concept doesn't apply only to employees—it can also apply to customers. Sometimes, a client or customer may not align with your values, and you have to move on from them.

For example, if a client berates your employees, swears at them, or treats them poorly, you, as a leader, must step in and say, *Look, the way you're speaking to my team member is not aligned with our values and principles. We don't stand for that.* This is just one example of how, as a leader, you must *live* the soundtrack—not only holding your team accountable to it but also holding customers, vendors, and third-party organizations accountable.

You have to communicate clearly: *This is how we do business. This is who we are. This is our identity.* That's incredibly important because, let's face it, some customers can be difficult. Sometimes, it's just their personality—they don't mean to be difficult; it's just how they communicate and interact. But there are times when, as a leader, you must recognize when a customer mistreats your employees—whether through unrealistic demands, burnout-inducing expectations, or degrading and abusive behavior. That is when you must step in and protect your team. In an earlier chapter, I talked about the importance of protecting your team. That responsibility doesn't just apply to what happens within the company—it also extends to external interactions. As a leader, you need to lead in *all* aspects of your organization.

This goes back to the earlier discussion about live performance. When you're on stage, stage presence matters. As a leader, you always have to show stage presence. It doesn't matter if you're on tour, playing a hundred arenas around the world—you still have to be that leader for your audience and your band. It doesn't matter what's going on in your life, how tired you are, or what challenges you face. If you see someone in the crowd throwing bottles or objects onto the stage that could injure one of your bandmates, you need to step up and take action.

I don't know if you've noticed, but lately, some artists have stopped their shows and said, "Look, if you throw one more thing on stage, we're going to stop the show." They're protecting themselves, but they're also protecting their band and their teammates. Sometimes, they ask security to remove the person from the venue: "Get them out of here. We don't want them as fans." That's part of being a leader, too.

It's amazing to see artists who truly care about others. Moments like that build trust and emotional attachment to a leader. That kind of leadership inspires and motivates people to help achieve the goals of a tour, a business, or any organization. It also highlights the human aspect of leadership—how people should genuinely treat each other and what behaviors should never be tolerated. True leadership means being willing to step up and fix what's wrong.

In some cases, standing by your principles can make you a stronger leader—even if it potentially costs you business. That's something to keep in mind. I remember hearing a story about a client who insisted that certain members of a firm be available and responsive 24 hours a day, seven days a week. The client would call at all hours of the day, including between the hours of 1 a.m. and 6 a.m., expecting someone to immediately pick up and respond to their needs. After a few early and unpleasant morning calls, the firm made the wise decision to move on from the client. The leaders in the firm decided that the well-being of their employees outweighed the fees they would have received from that client.

Another way of living the soundtrack is to always listen and ensure that your team is in tune. Everyone should be on board with what they're supposed to do. If you no longer hear your team talking about your values, mission, and purpose—perhaps the core principles are no longer resonating with them—then that's the moment when, as a leader, you need to step up. You need to keep the soundtrack alive, reinforce it with leadership, and ensure that people in every department understand it and why it's important. That is absolutely critical.

One of the most important things you can do as a leader is not just to tell people your values but to explain *why* they matter. *Why are these values important?* You should be able to tell your team, "Look, respect is one of our values because it defines how we treat others and our coworkers. It also sets clear boundaries for what we are not willing to tolerate. If you're going to be disrespectful, this is not the place for you. But if you treat everyone the right way and show respect for your teammates, you'll work better together. You'll be more aligned with the goals and objectives of the company. You'll focus more on the team rather than just your individual perspective." Make sure you emphasize *why*—why your mission is what it is, why your values are what they are, and why your purpose matters.

When it comes to bands and music, whatever that chemistry is—that magic, that drive that keeps you together—you can't lose sight of it. *What were our collective goals when we started this band? Why do we want to continue?* Whether you're in a band or a company, you have to constantly reflect on why your values are important. *Why did we do this? Why are we still together? Why does this matter to us and the people we serve?* Maybe you're questioning everything and thinking about quitting. But having those values and core principles in place can remind you not to quit because this is your mission. This is what you set out to do. You knew there would be challenges along the way, but staying committed to your mission ensures you push through and finish what you started.

Revisiting those core principles—reminding yourself and your team why you decided to move forward in the first place—keeps everyone on track. It helps you get out of ruts when you feel stuck. It helps you overcome obstacles. And most importantly, it keeps everyone on the same page.

I can't emphasize that enough for organizations because every organization will face headwinds. Every organization will encounter challenges.

There will always be disruptive people. There will be times when there doesn't seem to be a clear way forward. That's when everyone needs to come back to singing the same tune, living the soundtrack, and keeping that song alive. That soundtrack should always be playing in the background, reminding you, *As tough as this is, let's keep going.*

Let's make sure we finish what we started and do our best.

Exercise: *List three steps you can take to help your team live the soundtrack each day.*

You can use some of the examples I provided earlier in this chapter (e.g., signs, symbols, placards, computer wallpapers, t-shirts, coffee mugs), but really take the time to think about these steps. It's easy to say, *I'll just put a poster in the breakout room*—but why would you do that? Who will see it? Will it have the impact you want? What will the sign say? What color will it be? Will it stand out? You need to think through all these details to ensure each step you list has the impact you want to achieve.

Exercise: *What is your favorite movie soundtrack?*

There have been some great movie soundtracks over the years—*The Sound of Music, Saturday Night Fever, Purple Rain, O Brother, Where Art Thou?, Black Panther, Guardians of the Galaxy*—which one has resonated most with you, and why? With movie soundtracks, the music plays a significant role in emotionally connecting the viewer to what they see on screen. In many cases, hearing one song from the movie can immediately trigger memories of your favorite scenes or characters. What is it about the music that brings the movie alive? What is your favorite song from the soundtrack? One of my favorite movie soundtrack songs is "In the City" by Joe Walsh, from the movie *The Warriors*. It was the perfect song at the end of the movie, as the street gang, The Warriors, were walking along the beach into the sunset.

This is a fun exercise to reminisce about the movies that have had a significant musical impact on your life!

In the next chapter, we'll examine how leaders can stay relevant and inspiring over time using music principles to elevate team performance. Being creative in how leaders inspire and motivate their team is important to maintain chemistry. Since music universally connects us, it's a great way to keep your team jamming!

PART X
PILLAR TEN: KEEP INSPIRING —BE THE MUSIC TO YOUR TEAM'S EARS

19

THE MUSIC OF LEADERSHIP

One of the most important things a leader must do is stay relevant and inspiring over time. This is difficult, especially if you've been leading the team for a long time. We all tend to have certain things we like to say—quotes we rely on, familiar ways we try to motivate and inspire the team. But over time, those same quotes, statements, and efforts to inspire and motivate start to fall on deaf ears because you're essentially playing the same song over and over again.

In music, when you're leading a band and playing a lot of gigs—especially on a tight touring schedule or performing late at night—the band can start to wear down. Night after night, you have to bring the same energy and motivation. The songs may feel repetitive for you, but for the audience on that particular night in that particular city, it's their *first time* seeing you. They expect the same energy and excitement that every other audience has experienced throughout the tour.

The same applies to the band itself. Touring, practicing, writing—it can all become a grind. Over time, some band members may lose interest or grow tired of the same leadership principles or motivational tactics. So, how do you keep the team engaged? How do you motivate them to work hard, push through challenges, and stay committed to achieving the team's ultimate goals? Fatigue inevitably sets in, especially in organizations where the push never stops.

People start to feel exhausted, thinking, *Wow, I need a break*, or *I need something new to reenergize me.* This is where great leadership matters. A leader must listen to the team, observe their behaviors, and recognize the signs that motivation may be fading. Even if team members aren't expressing their fatigue verbally, their behaviors can indicate that what you're saying or doing isn't resonating anymore. You might see it in meetings—how they react when you introduce a topic or discuss an initiative. You might notice it in one-on-one conversations, in emails, or in their responsiveness. Their enthusiasm, engagement, or even the timing of their responses can indicate whether your motivational efforts are still effective.

As a leader, you must always be listening for these signs. You must recognize when team members—whether it's one, a few, or the entire group—are showing signs of fatigue or disengagement. Monitoring their energy levels ensures that what you're asking them to do is still something they have the will and motivation to accomplish.

I like to compare this to being a DJ. If you've ever DJ'd before, you know that when you're at the front of the room, playing music for an event, whether it's a wedding or a party, your goal is to keep the audience engaged. You want to keep them moving, riding the energy of each song. A great DJ knows how to mix things up—blending different songs, switching up beats and melodies, and keeping the crowd hyped, motivated, and energized.

It's amazing when you're at a party and the DJ keeps up the energy so well that you're still just as inspired and motivated to dance and have fun four hours in. But if you think about it, if the DJ played the *same* song for four hours, the room would probably start emptying quickly. Even if it's everyone's favorite song, hearing it on repeat would eventually lead to fatigue. People would start thinking, *Okay, I've heard this song enough. I need to hear something else. I need something new to keep me going.* And what will that next song be? A good DJ knows when to play the next song and which song will best complement the one that just finished. I'm sure we've all been at parties where, with each new song, we think, *Oh my God, this is a great song!* The energy just keeps building all night long.

As a leader, think of yourself as that DJ. You want to play the right songs. We talked about creating a soundtrack for your team to motivate and inspire them. We discussed five key songs for that purpose, but you may want to continue adding to that playlist. You may want to develop new leadership ideas, fresh ways to inspire your team, or new quotes that resonate.

Make sure that what you say, the quotes you use, and the principles you apply are relevant to the moment and the challenges your team is facing. When you deliver these messages, bring energy and motivation because it's not just *what* you say but *how* you say it. It goes back to the famous Maya Angelou quote: *People will forget what you said, people will forget what you did, but people will never forget how you made them feel.* Are you making your team feel inspired and motivated? Or is what you're saying falling on deaf ears? You have to constantly monitor this, ensuring that your words and actions create the effect you intend—just like a DJ.

If you want the crowd to slow dance, you'll lower the energy and play a slow jam that makes people want to grab their partner and be in the moment. But if you want them to get up and dance, you'll play something that inspires movement and excitement. In that sense, being a DJ is a bit like being a puppeteer. A great DJ can influence the crowd's energy simply by choosing the right music at the right time. Similarly, as a leader, you need to select messages and inspiration that resonate with your team. We've discussed the importance of listening to your team and finding bandmates who truly buy into your core principles. You want the under-lying soundtrack of those principles to always be playing, but you also want to add new songs—new messages—that inspire at the right time.

Another critical aspect of leadership is knowing *when* to introduce new ideas, quotes, or motivational messages. You have to monitor where your team is emotionally and mentally and then determine when would be a great time to lift them up, refocus them, and re-engage them in what you're trying to achieve.

Leaders cannot effectively communicate and inspire their team if they don't have a real connection with them. If they don't maintain an open line of communication or truly understand where their team is at, they will not be able to continue inspiring them.

If your teams are working on different parts of a collective goal—say the marketing team is developing a new campaign for an upcoming product launch while the product team is still finalizing features before it hits the market—it's essential that they communicate regularly. There needs to be an open line of communication so that each department knows what the others are doing.

This allows them to stay in tempo and in rhythm. It's similar to hearing a saxophone player perform a solo in a song you've practiced together. If I've heard the solo before, I know exactly when she will finish, and I'll be ready to transition into the next section of the song. That kind of communication—listening to what other groups are doing and staying in constant sync—ensures that everyone knows what to do next based on what they're hearing from another instrument, another team, or another department.

As a leader, use music to make things fun. Music has the power to motivate and inspire us—we all love it. So, why not think of leadership in a fun, engaging way? Imagine yourself as the leader of the band—because you are. How can you keep this cool and fun while ensuring everyone is playing the same song, staying harmonious in tempo and rhythm, and remaining in sync every day? It's a fun way for a leader to approach it— where it's not boring or mundane but rather interesting and engaging. Hopefully, based on the principles of the book, it will also resonate with the team.

It's also important for a leader to involve everyone in the process. You can even seek suggestions from your team. We've talked about open communication and feedback, so listen to what they have to say. Ask them: *I know we're going through some challenges right now. What ideas do you have to get things back on track?* You'd be surprised at the responses. Some leaders feel like they have to figure everything out on their own. They may worry that asking their team for input will be seen as a sign of weakness or that they don't know what they're doing. But I always say: "Great leaders serve the success of their team." Your goal is to help every person on your team succeed. When they succeed in their individual roles, the collective success of the team becomes that much greater. In those moments, timing is critical—what you say and when you say it matters.

Consider using principles from music to keep your team engaged. One of the most fun aspects of writing this book has been exploring the parallels between music and business—how so many principles of music apply to everyday life.

One of the most obvious is *harmony*. You want your team to be harmonious. Think about a choir—whether in church or elsewhere—where thirty people sing together, perfectly in sync. Every voice contributes to a beautiful, unified sound. Imagine if your team functioned the same way. Each person on your team has a unique role and responsibility. When everyone plays their part in harmony, the result is truly powerful. Everyone has their own voice, whether they're in accounting, legal, IT, or some other department of your organization. But you want those voices to work in harmony. You want all departments and the people within them to work together in the same pitch, tone, and timing to ensure that, collectively, the group is in sync.

Another important musical principle is *tempo*. You want your team to work at the right pace to achieve their goals. When setting goals—especially SMART goals—you need to make sure you're meeting them within the desired time frame.

This can be particularly challenging when you have many moving parts. Each component must work together to complete tasks on time and on budget. Then, the team must shift to the next task. As tasks are completed, you move closer to achieving the milestones you set together as a team. That's why it's critical to ensure that each piece functions cohesively and maintains the right tempo.

I've played live shows where the drummer was so hyped up that they started playing every song faster than usual. Since the drummer often sets the tempo—either by starting the song or counting it in—if they start too fast, it affects the entire band. The audience may not notice the difference, depending on how familiar they are with the song, but the faster tempo can throw off the band's rhythm because they're playing the song differently than they practiced it. When that happens, the music doesn't feel as *tight*, and it can impact the show's overall quality. This demonstrates how, if one part of your team is off rhythm, it can throw off the rest of the team as well. That's why it's essential to always listen and ensure everyone is in sync.

It's similar to an orchestra. You might hear a violinist performing a solo, but that solo is often a cue for a shift in the music—maybe even a tempo change. That transition has been carefully prearranged. Every instrument works harmoniously, allowing certain sections to lead transitions, set the mood, or shift the tempo. For example, a violin solo might end, and the horn section might come in seamlessly. That's exactly how it should work in business. As soon as one task is completed, the team should immediately transition to the next. This is where having a strategic plan is critical.

Think of your strategic plan as *sheet music*. When an orchestra plays a song, each musician reads from sheet music. If the *sheet music* represents your strategic plan, then each *transition in the song* represents a milestone in that plan. Each section of instruments corresponds to a department in your company:

- The horn section could be accounting.
- The strings could be technology.
- The bass section could be legal.
- The percussion section could be marketing.
- The conductor represents leadership.

Each instrument group plays its designated part—some for the entire song, some only at specific moments. But every musician knows *when* they're supposed to play, what *key* they're in, what *tempo* to follow, and how to transition smoothly—so that the song sounds seamless from beginning to end.

If one instrument group plays in a different key or misses a beat, it disrupts the song, and *everyone* can hear it. If one or more instrument groups don't have the sheet music—or are reading from different sheet music—that will also create chaos.

So, as a leader, make sure everyone on your team executes their part from the *same* plan, in the *same* key, and at the *same* tempo.

Another important element is *tone*, which is critical—especially as a leader—because you need to use the right tone with the people you work with. You want to communicate with the right tone to your team. I've worked with leaders who struggled to use the right tone to get their desired results. Often, these leaders relied on angry, forceful, or loud tones, resulting in them barking commands at their team. But as a leader, you have to *read the room*. Sometimes, your tone may not resonate with your team at that moment, and you need to recognize what tone will actually motivate them to perform at their best.

Some leaders rule by fear, and their tone reflects that. But ruling by fear can lead to other problems within your organization, such as retention issues, burnout, and low morale. Be mindful of your tone in every situation, ensuring that you use the right tone at the right moment to optimize performance and productivity.

You also want to operate as an *ensemble*. An ensemble is a group of musicians playing and singing together, working in harmony. Similarly, you need to ensure that all the moving parts of your team are working together for the group's collective success.

Of course, you also need to stay *in rhythm*. Rhythm is the foundation of music. No matter the genre, the rhythm is what gets you moving and feeling the music. Likewise, you want to ensure that the rhythm of your team is working and that your team feels connected to the beat of the organization.

If things are out of rhythm—if departments within your organization aren't effectively working together—it can disrupt team chemistry. As a leader, you need to stay focused on keeping every part of your team in sync. It's no different from a bandleader listening to all the instruments and being able to say, "Okay, I think the bass player is off rhythm" or "The guitar player is slightly ahead of the beat." Then, you make adjustments quickly to ensure that the song sounds the way it should.

Exercise: *Create a new message that you haven't used before to inspire and motivate your team.*

Consider incorporating some of the musical principles discussed in this chapter as you craft your message. Consider the *tone* you'll use, the *stories* you'll tell, and the *impact* your message will have.

The best time to write these types of motivational messages is when you have the mental space to reflect on them—not when things are already busy and chaotic. If you prepare these messages in advance, you'll have them ready when needed.

When an inspirational or motivational idea comes to you, write it down. Keep a list of powerful quotes, messages, and ideas that resonate with you. Whenever I see an inspirational quote I like or hear something that speaks to me, I write it down. Over time, I've built a list of these "nuggets" from books, conversations, and experiences. Then, when I need to inspire or motivate a team, I can pull from that collection and choose the right message for the right moment.

Create a system like this for yourself as a leader. That way, you'll always have a fresh, relevant message to inspire your team—using the musical principles we've talked about to keep them engaged and motivated.

> **Exercise:** *Create a list of the songs you identified in all the chapter exercises.*

This will become your personal leadership playlist. We've talked about your favorite songs, songs that inspire you, and songs you believe will motivate your team. Throughout the exercises, you've been asked to create different song lists. In this exercise, we're aggregating all those songs into one master playlist. This playlist will serve as a tool to motivate and inspire you and your team. It will help keep your team in rhythm, on track, and in harmony—ensuring that everyone sings the same tune and works toward the same goals.

Play these songs repeatedly to remind yourself of the lessons learned in this book. Ideally, when you hear the songs you wrote down in these exercises, they will trigger some of the key takeaways from earlier chapters.

In the final chapter, we'll explore how leaders can continue to raise the bar and strive to be better as a team. It's easy to become complacent after achieving success. How can you inspire your team to avoid the "one-hit" wonder trap and keep pushing to produce number-one hits?

20

THE PURSUIT OF EXCELLENCE

*W*e've covered a lot in this book, and now we've reached the final chapter. I intentionally structured this book to take you through the evolution of a band—an evolution that mirrors the growth of your team, your company, or your business.

We started with determining what genre you wanted to be in, what kind of product you wanted to create, and who your audience would be. You built your team with bandmates—hopefully the ideal ones—who could help you accomplish your company's goals and objectives.

You've practiced, performed, and jammed together, launched products together, and seen those products succeed. Now, you're managing stardom, and things are going well. Hopefully, as you apply the principles in this book to your business and the work you're doing today, you'll see success and position your company for even bigger and better things. That's the goal.

But the key is *maintaining* excellence. You've set a standard for your company; as a leader, it's your job to uphold that standard. You need to set the tone. The company's core principles are the guiding light that keeps everyone on your team aligned with its goals and objectives, maintaining excellence across all departments.

You really can't let *any* department falter. Earlier in the book, we discussed the importance of ensuring that every aspect of the client experience with your brand operates at a high level. You can't put out a great product but have poor customer service. Likewise, you can't have excellent customer service while offering a product with quality issues that weren't addressed before launch. All of these factors impact your audience as well as your team's morale and company culture.

As a leader, you ask a lot of your team. You expect every instrument to play in tune and in sync—all day, every day. Your team works together toward a common goal, but it's up to you to ensure everyone meets your set standards. This applies to longtime employees and to every new hire who joins your company. You want to ensure that everyone is operating at the same level of excellence.

But you don't want to get complacent. Complacency can be dangerous in any organization, especially when things are going well. You might think, *Okay, we've accomplished our initial goals, our products are selling well, and they're really popular right now—so maybe we can take our foot off the gas a little bit.* But the reality is, if everything is working in sync and the team is truly collaborating, then as a leader, you should be preparing them for new challenges. You should be preparing them for growth. You should be preparing them to *raise the bar.*

Two of the most important questions a leader should constantly ask their team are: "How can we be better? What can we do to improve upon what we've already accomplished?" These are great questions to ensure that the group doesn't become complacent—to prevent them from sitting back and thinking, *Okay, we've done what we needed to do, we're good now.* You want to instill a mindset of continuous improvement. Some musicians continue taking lessons even after they've *made it.* I've read that legendary guitarist Randy Rhoads continued to take guitar lessons even after reaching stardom with Ozzy Osbourne. No matter how good or successful you are, there are *always* ways to improve your craft.

And that's really the goal that leaders should strive for: How can we be better? How can we raise the level of quality, efficiency, innovation, and creativity? The beauty of teamwork is that the more you work together, the more you're in sync, the more chemistry you develop, and the more in tune you become—making it easier to identify areas for improvement. It's no different from a band that has already reached stardom but continues writing new songs. They may want to add another instrument, introduce a keyboard, or experiment with new sounds to expand their musical reach and fuel their creativity.

When you ask, "How can we be better?" seek input from your team, but then you take it one step further. If they say, "We can be better at meetings—we can be more efficient in planning them," ask them, "How would you do that? What steps would you take to make our meetings more efficient?" Get them involved in finding the answers to their own questions. That empowers them and gives them ownership, reinforcing that they are part of the process to raise the bar and set a higher standard. It also allows you to hear directly from them, gaining valuable feedback and insight into how they think things could be improved. The best part? You may hear ideas you hadn't even considered that could further elevate the team's performance.

As a team, you should ask these questions: How can we collaborate better? How can we allocate work more efficiently? How can we improve our products? How can we better serve our customers? You want to constantly think about how to improve, but you also need to raise the bar with realistic expectations.

There will be times when someone asks you to do something, and you think, *There's no way we can do that. It's impossible. That's completely unrealistic.*

I've been in situations where someone asked me to do the impossible—sound familiar? That kind of pressure can erode team chemistry and trust. If your team constantly feels like they are being asked to do the impossible, it will wear them down.

As a leader, it's your responsibility to ensure that what you ask of your team is realistically achievable. That doesn't mean you shouldn't push them—great leadership involves encouraging people to stretch beyond their comfort zones. But it also means understanding their strengths, workload, and limits. If you push too hard without awareness, you risk burnout, frustration, and a breakdown in trust.

Your team follows you because they believe in your vision and trust you to lead them there. When expectations become unrealistic, that trust begins to erode. They may start thinking, *We could work 24/7 and still not meet these demands.* That's a dangerous mindset to allow.

As mentioned earlier, leadership is about more than motivation—it's also about protection. You must know how far to push without jeopardizing morale or team chemistry. If your team starts questioning whether you truly understand what you're doing, your leadership becomes less effective.

Unrealistic expectations can lead your team to feel like their efforts are never enough. That's why setting clear, realistic, and sustainable goals is essential. Communication and feedback are critical—especially when the stakes are high—because your people need to know their work is seen, valued, and aligned with achievable outcomes.

You're only as successful as your team. If they're not in sync with one another, success will be difficult to achieve. Even though team members have their own unique roles, everything must work cohesively toward achieving your company's goals and objectives. Creating moments of inspiration, supporting each other as teammates, building a culture of innovation, and having a leader who helps guide the way—that's what makes success possible.

Maintaining transparency on your team is also important so that everyone understands what others are doing. When you're in a band playing live on stage, you can *hear* what the other instruments are doing. No one is hiding the bass line or the drumbeat—it's all there for the band to hear, allowing them to respond accordingly. Great bands that play together frequently develop an instinctive understanding of one another. They can almost anticipate what the others are going to do. A great example of this is improvisational jazz bands. I've seen many in my day, and they are incredible. They're so musically skilled that they can make up a song on the spot, simply jamming and playing off one another. They communicate through eye contact, subtle head nods, and occasional hand gestures.

But that level of coordination comes from knowing and listening to what the other person on your team is doing and then reacting to it. That's why transparency is so important. Each team member should be able to see how their efforts impact other departments and contribute to the goals and objectives of the organization. This understanding helps them see the significance of their role within the larger context of the company.

It's very similar to a musician on stage who is there to play lead guitar but is also listening to what the other musicians are doing. Because the music is transparent, they can hear how everything fits together. Maybe they add a guitar riff based on what the drummer or bass player just played, or they adjust based on the singer's phrasing or even how the audience is reacting: *This would be a great moment for a solo.* If you empower your team to listen, understand what's happening in other parts of the organization, and stay attuned to the bigger picture, they'll know how to react, respond, and grow—taking everything to a higher level.

Think about how you can raise the bar while maintaining the harmony you've already built within your team. Taking the time to think this through may help you avoid the "one-hit-wonder" trap in organizational growth. We talked about one-hit-wonder bands—every band wants a hit, but once they get one, it becomes, "What have you done for me lately? When's your next hit coming?" After achieving their first big hit, many bands spend the rest of their careers trying to find that second, third, or fourth hit. It's incredibly difficult. It's great when you accomplish something significant as a team—such as winning an award for your product, receiving industry recognition, or reaching a major milestone—but can you do it again? Now that you've found success, can your team stay intact? That's another challenge you have to anticipate.

You may have an incredible bass player in your band, and now that you've achieved stardom, other bands are thinking, *Wow, I'd love for that bass player to join us.* The same happens in business. You succeed, and suddenly, other companies start noticing your top talent. They may try to recruit your best programmers, designers, or strategists—offering them higher salaries or better benefits to lure them away.

You also have to evaluate whether your team still has the same drive and chemistry to create magic again. Sometimes, after reaching a big goal, you ease off the gas. You think, *We made it.* But the reality is, you still need that hunger to keep striving for greatness.

According to Billboard, there are only nine artists so far who have reached number one on the Billboard Hot 100 chart more than ten times. These artists include The Beatles, Rihanna, Drake, Taylor Swift, and Whitney Houston. Can you guess who has the most Number-one hits? The Beatles with 20. This is a phenomenal achievement and a testament to their drive and determination to keep raising the bar and pushing the boundaries of creativity.

Many artists spend their entire careers chasing *one big hit*. Some succeed, but most do not. Likewise, as businesses achieve success, they often expand —creating new product lines, building market share, and increasing brand awareness. But the question remains: *How can they keep putting out the hits?* I encourage you, as a leader, to follow the principles in this book to keep your team together—to keep your band playing great music, writing new songs, creating hit records, and performing at a level that continues to pack stadiums and engage audiences for years to come. If you stay true to your core principles—ensuring you have the right people on your team, listening to keep everyone in tune, making sure everyone is playing the same song, growing together, motivating and inspiring each other, fostering creativity, encouraging feedback and communication, and managing success as your organization scales—you will be able to sustain your momentum.

Following these principles will help you continue to raise the bar. It'll help you continue making hit records. Keep challenging each other, pushing each other to innovate, think outside the box, and find that next big hit. You never know when it's going to come.

And a lot of times, it takes a little magic. We talked about The Edge from U2 and how he described the magic that U2 creates when writing music—that's what you want. But you have to keep trying. You have to keep challenging yourself. You have to keep pushing yourself to be great and to be creative in order to reach that level and continue putting out hits that will keep your company thriving for years to come.

Also, put yourself in the shoes of the customer. Why would anyone want to buy your next album? Or in business, why would anyone want to continue buying your product or the next version of it? Keep thinking about that. These are the areas where you can continue to raise the bar and keep putting out hits that keep your company relevant.

Another important factor is empowering your team to keep lifting and motivating each other. That's also critical. It shouldn't all fall on the leader. A leader can motivate and inspire, but you should also have others on your team—especially senior members who have been with the group for a while—empowered to do the same for younger or newer team members.

A great leader has great generals—people who help reinforce the messaging, embody the core principles, and ensure that everyone is hearing and singing the same tune. They can also recognize when something is off and proactively address issues as they arise.

So it's not entirely on you as a leader, but rather, you create the environment that inspires, motivates, and empowers your team members to step in as needed to keep everyone in sync.

> **Exercise:** *What are your three biggest takeaways from this book that will help you continue to raise the bar in your organization?*

Reflect not only on the chapters in the book but also on your exercises. Look back at your answers—those might help spark insights into your three biggest takeaways. You may have already done the work in some areas, but if not, this is a great opportunity to pinpoint what in this book can help you improve as a leader. That is the whole goal of this book and why I wrote it.

At the end of the day, we're all trying to be better. Sometimes, we need guidance, principles, or simply a reminder. There may be things in this book that you've heard before, but hearing them again—especially in the context of music, where the concepts feel more engaging and fun—may be just what you need to take action. Maybe you'll think, *I've heard that before, but now I'm actually going to implement it and make sure my band is in tune and having fun.*

And you never know: your group will keep putting out hit records together, and you'll *enjoy* doing it. It won't feel like a grind. It won't become mundane or boring. People won't get complacent because they'll be chasing that next hit.

That desire for the next hit will be what inspires and motivates you. That same energy should drive you to keep improving—putting out better products, offering better service, listening better, and giving your audience exactly what they want.

So they continue buying your albums, coming to your shows, buying your merch, and engaging with you on social media. All of that should be part of what you're striving for.

CONCLUSION

The main message of my book is to develop core principles that you can use to grow your organization. It starts with identifying what type of leader you want to be. You may even use music as inspiration or motivation to help define your leadership style. Then, it's time to think about your mission.

What is your product? What is your business? What are you bringing to the world? This process gives you the opportunity to shape your team and build the right people around you to accomplish your goals and objectives, ensuring that they align with the core principles you've set forth. That alignment will help you become a better leader, not only in managing your team and developing chemistry and trust but also in understanding what drives them. It will help you inspire your team, encourage creativity and innovation, and use that innovation to improve your products, services, and brand presence.

Bringing the band together means ensuring that core principles define what is expected of your team—how they treat each other, interact with customers, and make decisions that align with the company's goals and objectives. These principles help create a cohesive, harmonious group, allowing your organization to thrive.

Once you've developed and launched a product, how do you manage that success? How do you keep your team engaged and motivated? How do you deal with conflict? How do you navigate chaos and crisis? How do you refine your efficiency as a team, manage growth, and scale your organization to where it needs to be? And once you succeed, how do you keep your team on the same page—singing the same tune, staying motivated to get better, raising the bar, and striving to do even greater things together? How do you overcome new challenges in a way that is fulfilling for everyone on the team? The key is ensuring that your team fully buys into what you're building, celebrates wins together, and continues growing as a team and an organization. Most importantly, how do *you* continue growing as a leader—becoming the best version of yourself to serve both your team's success and the organization's overall success?

You are the maestro, the lead singer, the conductor, if you will. You are the leader. It's up to you to pull it all together. It's up to you to ensure that the band is ready for every show, every opportunity, every challenge, and every road trip—whatever it may be. You are the one who must maintain a constant voice and a constant presence on stage.

And no matter what happens, you remain in control. You stay true to your core principles. You continue to inspire and motivate, whether you're experiencing success or facing setbacks. You are prepared for it all because you've built your foundation on the principles we've discussed.

So embrace the role. Be the leader you want to be. Be authentic. Be present. And support your team in every way you can.

I sincerely thank everyone for reading this book. This has truly been a passion project for me—something I've wanted to create for a long time. It's inspired not only by my deep connection to music and how it has motivated me over the years but also by the incredible people I meet everywhere I go. I'm constantly running into leaders, executives, and other professionals who want to share their stories or talk about their own connection to music. It's truly amazing.

I hope there are many people out there like me—executives, leaders, or professionals who have experienced some level of success yet still share a deep passion for music. Music has shaped moments in our lives, strengthened friendships, and fostered connections with colleagues. It has helped build something special—like a great band that makes it big, releases a number-one hit, and suddenly finds itself touring the world, living the dream.

This book aims to help you get there, and I truly hope you can.

I also hope you continue to revisit the principles in this book and live by them. *Playing on repeat* is essential—reinforcing these ideas, constantly thinking about them, and finding new ways to improve. Maybe you'll even come up with new "songs" to inspire and guide your team to where they need to be.

All of this is possible. If you follow the principles in this book, you *can* get there. And more importantly, you can have fun doing it—with your team. They are your band. Keep making great music together, and keep your customers jamming to your sound for years to come.

As I was writing this book, my goal was for you to experience the same feeling you get when listening to your favorite song. I hope I've accomplished that.

Thank you!

THANK YOU FOR READING MY BOOK!

The Soundtrack of Leadership Community
This QR code leads to a paid online community to connect with me and other leaders who share a passion for music. People who purchase the book will receive one month free.

The Soundtrack of Leadership - Exercises and Workbook
This QR code leads to a workbook that includes all of The Soundtrack of Leadership exercises and space to answer questions, take notes, and reflect thoughts.

Five Leadership Lessons I Learned from Playing In a Band (BONUS VIDEO)

This QR code leads to a video of me providing five leadership lessons I learned from playing in a band.

I appreciate your interest in my book and value your feedback as it helps me improve future versions of this book.
I would appreciate it if you could leave your invaluable review on Amazon.com with your feedback.
Thank you!

www.ingramcontent.com/pod-product-compliance
Lightning Source LLC
Chambersburg PA
CBHW031502120626
46545CB00005B/1719